Special Stories for Disability Awareness

by the same author

Disability Voice
Towards an Enabling Education
ISBN-13: 978 1 85302 355 2   ISBN-10: 1 85302 355 8

of related interest

Special Brothers and Sisters
Stories and Tips for Siblings of Children with a Disability or Serious Illness
Edited by Annette Hames and Monica McCaffrey
ISBN-13: 978 1 84310 383 7   ISBN-10: 1 84310 383 4

The Adventures of the Little Tin Tortoise
A Self-Esteem Story with Activities for Teachers, Parents and Carers
Deborah Plummer
ISBN-13: 978 1 84310 406 3   ISBN-10: 1 84310 406 7

Classroom Tales
Using Storytelling to Build Emotional, Social and Academic Skills across the Primary Curriculum
Jennifer M. Fox Eades
ISBN-13: 978 1 84310 304 2   ISBN-10: 1 84310 304 4

Drama Therapy and Storymaking in Special Education
Paula Crimmens
ISBN-13: 978 1 84310 291 5   ISBN-10: 1 84310 291 9

Challenge Me!™
Mobility Activity Cards
Amanda Elliott
ISBN-13: 978 1 84310 497 1   ISBN-10: 1 84310 497 0

Self-Esteem Games for Children
Deborah M. Plummer
ISBN-13: 978 1 84310 424 7   ISBN-10: 1 84310 424 5

No More Stinking Thinking
A Workbook For Teaching Children Positive Thinking
Joann Altiero
ISBN-13: 978 1 84310 839 9   ISBN-10: 1 84310 839 9

Chasing Ideas
The Fun of Freeing Your Child's Imagination
Revised Edition
Christine Durham
ISBN-13: 978 1 84310 460 5   ISBN-10: 1 84310 460 1

Brotherly Feelings
Me, My Emotions, and My Brother with Asperger's Syndrome
Sam Frender and Robin Schiffmiller
ISBN-13: 978 1 84310 850 4   ISBN-10: 1 84310 850 X

Special Stories for Disability Awareness

Stories and Activities for Teachers, Parents and Professionals

Mal Leicester

Illustrations by Taryn Shrigley-Wightman

Jessica Kingsley Publishers
London and Philadelphia

First published in 2007
by Jessica Kingsley Publishers
116 Pentonville Road
London N1 9JB, UK
and
400 Market Street, Suite 400
Philadelphia, PA 19106, USA

www.jkp.com

Library of Congress Cataloging in Publication Data

Leicester, Mal.
  Special stories for disability awareness : stories and activities for teachers, parents, and professionals / Mal Leicester.
    p. cm.
  Includes bibliographical references.
  ISBN-13: 978-1-84310-390-5 (pbk.)
  ISBN-10: 1-84310-390-7 (pbk.)
  1. Children with disabilities--Attitudes. 2. Values--Study and teaching (Elementary)--Activity programs. 3. Storytelling. I. Title.
  HV888.L453 2007
  362.4--dc22

                    2006022135

British Library Cataloguing in Publication Data
A CIP catalogue record for this book is available from the British Library

ISBN-13: 978 1 84310 390 5
ISBN-10: 1 84310 390 7

Printed and bound in Great Britain by
Printwise (Haverhill) Ltd, Suffolk

Contents

Acknowledgements

As always thanks are due to Karen Langley for her secretarial assistance. I am also deeply grateful to Catherine Twelvetrees for invaluable help in the preparation of the manuscript and for so competently working to a tight timescale. Finally I want to express my appreciation to Roger Twelvetrees and the Nottingham Trent writers for their perceptive comments on the stories.

Introduction: Understanding Disability

In this book I have provided stories in which the heroes and heroines are disabled children, with associated learning activities to promote disability awareness at Key Stages 1 and 2 in England and Wales (4–11 years) and an exploration of the issues implicit in each story for any teacher, parent or professional working with primary school children.

To understand disability issues is important for anyone who cares about children and who has some responsibility for their cognitive and emotional development. Thus parents and other carers, teachers in special and mainstream schools, learning specialists, psychologists, speech, occupational and physical therapists and leaders of children's voluntary clubs and organisations all need disability awareness and should nurture this kind of understanding in 'their' children – disabled and non-disabled alike.

The nature of story

In each of the following chapters I have used the *power of story* as a gateway into greater understanding of the *experiences* of disabled children. Stories help us to understand our own experiences and those of others, providing access to inner thoughts and feelings. Thus they readily provide a springboard into greater disability awareness, both at a cognitive level and through deeper empathy at an emotional level. In addition, they implicitly endorse values of compassion and justice.

Storytelling has always been a powerful and basic human activity. In all civilisations and cultures, both the activity of storytelling and significant, individual stories have been passed down the generations. This is because, long before the printed word was available, story was the means by which people attempted to make sense of their experience of the world, to communicate that understanding and to achieve a collective wisdom through passing on accumulating *knowledge and values* in a memorable and accessible way.

Stories both *educate and entertain*. We learn from them and the learning is fun. They also stimulate our imagination and thus our own creativity. Moreover, because children enjoy stories, they simultaneously learn to love learning.

Crucially, stories explore even painful emotions in an enjoyable way. The children in these stories face fear, loss, anxiety, feeling 'different', name-calling, bullying, exclusion – as well as joy, success, friendship and emotional growth. Because these experiences are explored in stories, ones in which the reader can readily identify with the child protagonist, the painful emotions (aspects of any child's world) are faced in a safe and manageable context.

Story and disabled children

Stories in which the hero or heroine is a disabled child are scarce. This collection addresses this yawning gap in children's reading experiences and thus meets a crucial educational need. We know that the books we read as children influence our developing attitudes and values, as well as promoting our knowledge and understanding of the world. It is surely important that all children see disabled child heroes and heroines actively solving problems in a whole variety of contexts and situations.

Disabled children need and deserve to see that disabled characters are included in the world of books. (Disabled children will enjoy reading much more if they can read about children who share their impairment.) They need to identify with characters who share their experiences and who boost their self-esteem. The children in the stories provide positive role models for children with a variety of impairments. These children and their parents want to see non-stereotyped disabled people included – as valued members of society.

It is equally important that non-disabled children read stories with disabled characters. The omission of such characters carries an implicit message that they are less interesting and less valued. Such messages affect the children's developing attitudes and beliefs. We know that even very young children tend to develop prejudiced attitudes towards people 'different' from themselves, and may bully the vulnerably 'different'. Inclusion in stories helps to counter this prejudice. In several of the stories in the collection, the disabled child faces overt prejudice, for example, Jack in 'A Kind Revenge', or indirect prejudice, for example Charlotte in 'Across the Pond'. Non-disabled children need the opportunity to develop, through the power of story, an empathy with 'difference' of *this kind*.

Some of the disabled children in these stories are from minority ethnic groups (e.g. Charlotte in 'Across the Pond' is African–Caribbean and Ravi in 'Gifts for Divali' is Asian). Such children also face prejudice based on colour and culture. In other words disabled, black children face endemic social prejudice and discrimination on, as it were, two 'exclusion' frontiers. It is important that material for children is permeated by cultural diversity, and since the movement to multicultural education some decades ago, children's literature has increasingly become so permeated. Over time children's literature has become more appropriate for our multicultural society. Children with the full range of ethnic and cultural backgrounds are now in character-led stories. It is surely also important that diversity and inclusion in children's reading is similarly permeated by disabled characters, disabled awareness and disabled experience.

The eight stories in this book include two children with sensory impairments, two with a mobility impairment, two with learning difficulty/difference and three who have experienced emotional and behavioural distress. Their experiences, for example being lost, losing something valued, looking 'different' in some way, name-calling, quarrels, interdependence, exclusion, gift giving and receiving, and friendship, are *universal* experiences. In other words, they are experiences of both disabled and non-disabled children. The stories show these *shared* experiences, but also illuminate the particular resonance and significance they have for the disabled child in the story.

Positive perspectives

Models of disability

There are positive and negative perspectives on disability and a good starting point for disability awareness is to move away from negative perspectives which see disability as 'illness' or 'tragedy' and generate pity rather than genuine recognition of rights and equality. The model of disability which locates disability with the individual person – his or her 'illness', 'problem', 'tragedy' – has been called the *medical model*. It is contrasted with the much more positive *social model* which locates disability in a restricting environment. This perspective underpins the 'disability rights' movement. The experiences of disabled people are of social restrictions in the world around them. The individual's experience of disability is created in interactions with a physical and social world designed for non-disabled living.

A distinction could be made here between 'disability' and 'impairment'. The degree to which an individual's impairment restricts his or her life (disables him or her) is largely *socially* conditioned. We see the importance of social environmental factors in several of the stories, e.g. 'Tom's Famous Bridge' (Tom's guide dog); 'The Magic Shoe Box' (the imposition of an inflexible and insensitive 'uniform'); 'Signs of Change' (the initial lack of signing in Amy's school). The social model encourages social interaction based on notions of equal rights with social policy and provision based on these rights (on an appropriate educational support in a mainstream school for Amy, for example). The individual or medical model encourages social interactions based on pity with social policy geared towards charitable compensation.

Of course, the stories also show that the experiences of disabled people are, as for all people, complex and varied and do include experiences of personal tragedy, pain and frustration. A positive perspective which integrates the personal (highly individual nature of experience) and the political (social aspect of experiencing unnecessary restrictions) is true to lived experience.

Common stereotypes

The characters of the children in the stories work against the common disability stereotypes. Such stereotypes include:

- The pitiable or noble alternative – Amy, in 'Signs of Change' is shown to be neither pitiable nor particularly 'brave'.

- A victim – Jack, in 'A Kind Revenge', finds a way to 'fight' back.

- Evil – we see that the twins in 'One and One Make Trouble' are not intending to be troublesome, and Max in 'The Careless Boy' is capable of coming to care.

- Freaks/laughable – understanding Ravi in 'Gifts for Divali' ensures that we will not mistakenly perceive him in these negative ways.

- Burden – In 'Tom's Famous Bridge' we see that if provided with a stick/guide dog, Tom is well able to cope with difficult situations.

- Chip on shoulder – In 'Across the Pond' we understand why Charlotte responds sharply to Liza-Marie's initial question. For her it was yet another experience of prejudice and potential discrimination.

- Incapable of participation in daily life – In 'The Magic Shoe Box' it was the unnecessary demand for lace-up shoes, not Ellie's impairments, that made participation in school life a problem.

How to use this book

This book has a focus on disability and disability awareness and is intended for use by teachers in England and Wales; the material will be appropriate for teaching children at both Key Stages 1 and 2, which roughly translates to children aged 4–11. It provides well-planned learning sessions with photocopiable pages, lovely illustrations and structured learning activities which children enjoy.

In each chapter, after every story and linked to it, these learning activities are divided into four categories:

Category A provides enjoyable 'Circle Time' games, questions and discussion. The children form a circle which should come to feel a secure, inclusive space in which they can explore shared issues and problems and feelings. As Jenny Mosley and Pat Murray have written:

> The circle has always been a symbol of unity, healing and power. Many cultures have roots in the problem-solving, goal-achieving potential of the circle. The North American Indians used to sit in a circle with their talking object, often a feather or a pipe. Whoever was talking while holding the pipe would not have his train of thought interrupted by others in the circle. (*Quality Circle Time in the Primary Classroom*, 1996, p.70)

Circles have no top or bottom and symbolically contain rather than exclude. They work well for games and discussions aiming to enhance children's self-confidence and self-esteem; they also provide an experience of group participation and of democratic problem solving. The children develop discussion skills, democratic values and greater interpersonal understanding with other group members.

Category B provides 'awareness activities'. These promote children's understanding of disability issues and their empathy with disabled children, sometimes through imaginative identification and sometimes through the provision of experiential learning.

Category C provides 'Fun things to make and do'; things linked in some way to the stories. The children will enjoy making these poems, stories, pictures and objects, and the underlying values and implicit 'message' are positive and inclusive.

Category D is a suggestion or suggestions for a poster to make together. This endorses the value of *co-operation* and the 'message' of our *interdependence*. In several cases it will also provide a more permanent record of the understandings gained in the foregoing session.

Flexibility

Each chapter provides a story, linked discussion and a selection of associated learning activities. One story, with discussion and one or two of the follow-up activities, provides one complete session. You could work through the *remaining* activities before moving to the next chapter or, alternatively, move straight through from Chapter 1 to Chapter 8 and subsequently re-visit the stories, choosing a different selection of the activities provided.

The intention is to save you time by providing well-structured and disability-aware material for use with the children. The sequence and timing can be varied to suit you.

The sessions

- Having introduced the theme of the story you can tell *or* read it.

- The children could sit in a circle for the story and discussion time.

- Deal with 'difficult' vocabulary in your usual way. This often means explaining words as you come to them in the story. Introduce some of the vocabulary as the children colour the picture provided.

- You may or may not want to ask the *closed* (comprehension-type) questions to check understanding. You may want to ask some of them as you read, or only after you have finished reading, or not at all.

- You can select or add to the more *open* 'points for discussion' – according to those aspects of the theme most relevant to your children.

- You can select or add to the suggested activities. Some activities could be used in follow-up sessions.

- You can link the themes with each other and with other on-going projects. For example, the story, theme and activities in Chapter 1 connect with animals/pets projects, Chapters 3 and 8 with anti-bullying initiatives, Chapter 5 with language awareness, Chapter 6 with multicultural education; and the stories in Chapters 2–8 all feature different *family* structures.

- Teaching that accommodates a particular child's disability will very often be 'good practice' for all children.

Additional considerations for teachers in schools

Language and literacy

As well as having a particular focus on disability, given the valuing of story and discussion, each session contributes to the children's language development. Key skills in English/literacy such as speaking, listening, reflecting, critical thought, reasoning and concentrating are involved. In addition, several activities involve art and craft work and one or two highlight numeracy.

Values education

The collection as a whole makes a contribution to values education. The stories, discussion and activities all encourage children to unlearn disablist prejudice and to develop positive attitudes to themselves and others.

This particular aspect of values education (attitudes and disability) is relatively neglected, in spite of some increase in the inclusion of disabled children in mainstream schools. This resource will make a contribution to developing more successful inclusion – for example, through dealing with bullying and developing a welcoming and inclusive ethos.

Age levels

The material is intended for use at Key Stages 1 and 2 in England and Wales. Since this includes a relatively wide age range (4–11 years), use the material at the developmental level appropriate for your children. A class of younger children may 'tell' rather than 'write' their own stories and learn to recognise key words. Older children, on the other hand, will be able to write their own associated stories and poems and may even take a turn in reading part of the theme story.

Precious time

The book is intended to be a useful and *time-saving* resource for home, classroom and elsewhere. I am sure that, like all learning/teaching resources, it will be used in a whole variety of different ways. Some may reach for the book as the basis for a morning's work on those (rare but inevitable!) occasions when they simply have not had time to prepare material of their own. Others may take each story/activity as the starting point for an extended project on the highlighted theme. Schools may wish to use the resource in a whole-school approach to values education. They may encourage parents to use the book to work with their child. The book could provide bedtime or rainy-day stories with the bonus of discussion points and associated educational activities. In particular, it should enrich Circle Time and literacy work. In whatever way you choose to use it, I hope that you and the children will enjoy the theme-stories and the activities, and that these will genuinely promote the development of those worthwhile values, skills and attitudes which are part of a balanced, 'disability aware' education.

1

Tom's Famous Bridge

Background notes

The child in the story

Tom is 14 years old. He has been blind from birth. He attends a school for visually impaired children. Fortunately the school is situated near his home which means he can attend as a day pupil. He lives at home with his mum and dad. Like many children who have a dog, Tom is devoted to Scamp, who in turn is devoted to Tom. Tom is an intelligent, popular boy. He plays the drums exceptionally well. He is in the school orchestra and practises every day.

Additional points

- In this story we see that Tom makes keen use of his senses of hearing and touch. Though he cannot see, he is seen to be an able child.

- In this story Tom has a guide dog. In the UK, the major organisations do not normally provide guide dogs for children under 16. Tom's mum, we assume, has found a small provider who, in this particular case, was prepared to do so.

- Many non-disabled and disabled children will have experienced some of Tom's experiences – being lost, loving their dog, making music – experiences heightened by Tom's blindness.

Awareness issues implicit in the story

1. Abilities and disabilities

We each have abilities and disabilities. How much our disabilities are a problem depends on the environment. (Recognition of this is known as 'the social model' of disability). Fog is not a handicap for Tom but, without a guide dog, not having sounds at a pedestrian crossing might be.

Try to help the children to understand three things connected with this:

- We all have abilities and disabilities.

- We can be disabled in one thing (e.g. sight) and not in others (e.g. hearing, reasoning, memory, mobility).

- His or her environment and the people in that environment can help or hinder someone who has impairments (such as being visually impaired, deaf or a wheelchair user).

2. The location of school

Tom lives near his school but many disabled children have a long journey to and from their special school. They are bussed out of their neighbourhood and away from siblings and neighbourhood children. Some children live too far away even for daily travel and in term time must live away from home.

The more that neighbourhood schools can be truly inclusive, the greater the number of disabled children who would not need to experience this educational apartheid.

3. The importance of a pet

Many children enjoy having a pet and disabled children can benefit enormously from having one (especially, where this is possible, a dog). Pets don't judge us as 'different', call us names, exclude or bully or patronise. They boost our self-esteem and our well-being, and give love and fun. Moreover, we all want to be 'the helper', sometimes, rather than 'the helped'. Disabled children often enjoy looking after, or helping to look after their (or the family or school) pets.

4. The story experience: being lost

Many children have experienced being lost. They have experienced fear, panic and 'aloneness' until they are found. They will be able to identify with

Tom's feelings about Scamp being lost and about when Tom himself was lost. Sighted children may imagine that being blind would feel like being lost in the dark. You can readily generate sympathy for blind people, but try to generate willingness to be helpful without patronisation. Tom does not feel fear and 'aloneness' from his lack of sight but, like any of us would, he was glad of Mum's help in searching for Scamp.

5. The importance of the senses

Sight is a key sense for human beings. Perhaps that is why we use much sight-based vocabulary, e.g. 'I see' for 'I understand'. Blind people also use this vocabulary. Stimulate the children's awareness that we learn about the world through our senses – sight, hearing, touch, taste, smell. Becoming more conscious about colours, shapes, sounds, textures, scents, and so on will feed their creativity in the visual arts, music and literature. This story is a useful springboard into creative activity (drawing on the senses) to encourage the children's creative development.

Further reading

Hull, J.M. (1990) *Touching the Rock: An Experience of Blindness.* London: The Sheldon Press.

Leicester, M. (1998) *Disability Voice: Towards an Enabling Education.* London: Jessica Kingsley Publishers.

Swain, J., French, S., Thomas, C. and Barner, C. (eds) (2004) *Disabling Barriers – Enabling Environments.* Oxford: OUP.

Storytelling notes

Using the story

As the storyteller, it's likely that you will instinctively structure the timing of the story to provide the children with interesting activities, and will thereby offer them opportunities for stimulation and learning. The plan below is a guide to using the story in an active way, and need not be followed in exactly the sequence that follows – be as creative and flexible with the activities as you like.

Story themes

There are several themes in the story: you could focus on 'the five senses', 'pets', 'guide dogs', 'the experience of blindness' (for Tom).

1. *Introduce the story and theme.* The story is about Tom who is blind. In the story he makes good use of his sense of hearing. What are the five senses people have? (sight, hearing, touch, smell, taste).

2. *Vocabulary.* Make sure the children understand the words. Introduce some of these as they colour the picture, and introduce some in context – as you come to them in the story.

3. *The story.* Show the illustration and tell or read the story.

4. *Talking about the story.* Use some of the questions and discussion points given, and some of your own, to stimulate the children to talk about the story.

5. *Fun activities for active learning.* The activities include Circle Time games and discussion, things to make, including a co-operative poster for everyone to make together, and 'awareness' activities.

Introduce the story and theme

- We are all good at some things and not at others. Tom can't see. Notice, in the story, all the things he can do.

- We can be helpful to people who are blind or partially sighted. Notice, in the story, how Tom's mum helps Tom.

- We should not offer help that people don't need. How can we tell? If we can't tell, a friendly question (would you like me to…) will seldom offend.

Vocabulary

You can introduce some vocabulary as the children colour in the relevant picture, e.g. guide dog, harness, fur, training. (Pictures can be found in Appendix Two.)

Use your usual ways of introducing new words.

pounded – to beat (e.g. on a drum)

velvety – like velvet (smooth and soft)

released – let free

direction – the way to go

circular – in a circle

whimpered – small cry (e.g. of a dog)

anxious – worried

disappeared – not able to be found

bewildered – confused

desperately – extremely, anxiously (keen to find Scamp)

familiar – usual

coaxed – persuaded

The story: Tom's Famous Bridge

Tom pounded his drums. *If thunder could dance*, he thought, *it would sound like this.*

'Time for some air, Scamp,' he said at the end.

Scamp thumped his tail against the floor. 'Thump. Thump. Thump.'

Tom climbed the stairs from the basement. The wooden rail felt round and smooth under his hand. Behind him he heard the click of Scamp's claws on the steps. Tom opened the door into the garden. He was aware of a brightening. He lifted his face to the warm rays of the sun. He felt Scamp push past him and smiled. He managed perfectly well with his stick. He hadn't wanted a guide dog. But Mum had insisted.

'Since you're determined to go places on your own, Tom, a dog will help.'

Well, Tom must admit he was glad now. Scamp was such a great dog. The best! He was a Labrador with a smooth coat. Tom often tickled him behind his velvety ears, which he loved. Mum said Scamp was black, which is very dark, but with a bright mark on his forehead.

Though lost in these thoughts, Tom heard Mum come up behind him.

'Just look at the energy of that dog,' she said. 'Shall we take him up the brook?'

'Yeah,' said Tom. 'He likes it there.'

At the fields Tom released Scamp, and listened to him snuffing about as they walked. They reached the bridge over the brook and he heard Scamp splash into the water. He threw stones for Scamp to retrieve.

'A good way to give him a bath,' Mum said.

Tom tried to keep out of the way when Scamp shook the water from his fur, but felt the wet drops spatter his hand and his face.

'Remember when you led Alex over this bridge?' Mum said, and Tom laughed.

The day had been foggy and Alex and his mum had been scared to go over. There were no rails and they couldn't see a thing. Tom had found them there, stuck.

'Hang on to me,' he'd said. 'Like in the conga. I go over this bridge every day with my stick,' and he'd led them across. The story had whispered round the neighbourhood like a breeze and even reached the local paper. For a few weeks Tom had been a local hero, which had been nice.

'In fact, it should be called 'Tom's Famous Bridge,' Mum said.

Tom and Mum turned in the direction of home, taking a circular route through a small wood.

'I think you and Scamp could do the walk on our own tomorrow, Tom,' Mum said.

Tom was quiet for a moment. He really wanted to go on his own, just him and Scamp, but secretly he was scared of losing his dog.

'OK,' he said at last.

'Take your stick for when Scamp's out of the harness. And your mobile phone – just in case.'

⋆   ⋆   ⋆

So, the next morning, after drum practice, when Tom took Scamp for his usual walk, there was just the two of them. Once they reached the fields, Tom released Scamp, but he felt anxious. It was the first time Tom had been on his own with Scamp out of the harness. The dog bounded about, coming back to sniff Tom's hand, cold nose on warm skin, whenever Tom called him, which was very frequently! Eventually they reached the brook.

'You can have a longer splash today, Scamp,' Tom said.

He threw lots of stones for his dog and began to feel more relaxed. After Scamp's play-bath they walked on to the woods. They both enjoyed it there. Scamp ran from tree to tree sniffing and Tom listened to Scamp and to the singing birds. Into this peaceful scene, like an unexpected thump on the nose, a roll of thunder crashed directly overhead and rain poured down in a sudden summer storm. Tom heard Scamp whimper as he bolted away.

'Scamp,' Tom called urgently. He listened. All he could hear were the sounds of the rain. There was no sound of his dog.

'Scamp,' Tom yelled, increasingly worried, but still the dog didn't return. Tom's worst fear had come true.

Tom hurried home. That day, as always, the differing sounds of the rain were a guide to the objects around him, but in his hurry, Tom stumbled several times on the wet grass. He was scared that Scamp, in a panic to get home, might dash into the road and in front of a car.

But Scamp hadn't gone home. He wasn't there. Mum and Tom went back to the fields, to search for him.

They followed their usual route, over the fields, across the bridge, back through the woods. Tom knew that Mum was looking out for Scamp, and he called for him every step of the way. Sadly, Scamp had completely disappeared.

'Let's circle back one more time,' said Mum. 'At least the storm has passed.'

Tom held Mum's arm over the squelchy ground, his mind in turmoil – like the storm was raging inside his head. He called out for Scamp constantly, feeling sick with worry. If only they hadn't gone for that walk! How could he bear to lose his best friend? Tom remembered getting lost himself. It was only a short time but it had felt like forever. He had wandered about bewildered and scared and feeling so alone. He hadn't known what would happen to him, how he could get food or somewhere to sleep. His heart ached for his dog.

Mum stopped by the bridge to scan the field beyond.

'Scamp,' Tom called, desperately. 'Scamp! Scamp!'

Faintly he heard a familiar 'thump, thump, thump.'

'Listen,' he said.

They stood, silently.

'I can't hear anything,' said Mum. 'Did you hear him bark?'

'No. Listen. When I call him,' said Tom.

'Scamp! Scamp!' he called again.

Once more Tom heard it. 'Thump, thump, thump.'

'His tail,' he said. 'He thumps his tail when he hears his name.'

'Scamp!' he called loudly.

'Thump, thump, thump.'

'I still can't hear anything,' said Mum.

'Under the bridge. Mum, he's under the bridge.'

'Wait here, Tom,' she said.

He heard Mum scramble down to the stream.

'There you are,' he heard her say. 'Were you frightened, Scampie, poor boy? There, there then.'

'Is he alright?' Tom shouted.

'He's fine,' Mum replied. 'Just a bit scared. He's hiding under the bridge to one side of the water. He's scared to come out. Call to him, darling.'

'Come on, Scamp. Good boy,' Tom coaxed. 'Come on. Good boy,' and like sunshine after rain, happiness warmed his whole body when Scamp's wet nose touched his hand. The dog was trembling and Tom tickled behind his ears and stroked him gently until he was still.

After that they went home and the following week Scamp began more training, to get him used to sudden loud noises. Out on the fields, though, Tom was no longer scared. He was no longer worried about losing his dog. At least he would know now where to find Scamp if it happened again. He would be hiding, under 'Tom's famous bridge'.

Talking about the story

Did the children understand:

- what Tom was good at?
- how Tom's mum helped on their walks?
- what Tom did one foggy day?
- how Tom knew where Scamp was hiding?
- where Scamp was hiding?

Points for discussion

- What is the story about? (e.g. being lost; a guide dog; love for a pet... etc. The children should understand there is not just one right answer.)

- What do you like to look at? (Suggest some of your own favourite things as examples, e.g. rainbows, butterflies.)

- What are some of your favourite sounds? (e.g. music, rain, the sea.)

- What senses did Tom use to find out about the world?

- Tom was good at drumming. What are you good at? (Join in this to build each child's self-esteem – point out what children who have not spoken up for themselves are good at.)

Resources

The children could look through their books, or through a story, or poetry or song anthology to find other relevant stories, poems, rhymes, songs. (They could be about pets, the senses, music, thunder, being lost, sounds, etc.)

STORIES

Leicester, M. (2004) 'One Step Ahead.' In *Stories for Inclusive Schools: Developing Young Pupils' Skills*. London: Routledge/ Falmer. The story of how Tom led his friend across the bridge on a foggy day.

Tomlinson, J. (2004) *The Owl Who Was Afraid of the Dark: Sing a Story*. London: Egmont Books Ltd.

POEMS

Farjeon, E. (1979) 'Sounds in the Evening.' In J. Foster (ed.) *A First Poetry Book*. Oxford: OUP, p.18. The same anthology has three excellent poems about dogs: 'Bones' (B. Lee); 'Greedy Dog' (J. Hurley); 'Roger the Dog' (T. Hughes).

Kitching, J. (1984) 'Dogs.' In J. Foster (ed.) *A Very First Poetry Book*. Oxford: OUP.

Children might like to learn and chant this traditional rhyme:

I hear thunder
I hear thunder
So do you
So do you

Pitter-patter raindrops
Pitter-patter raindrops
I'm wet through
So are you.

They could chant in synchrony with one child (or group) chanting one line behind the other(s).

Fun activities for active learning

Circle Time

- Circle Time game: Feel and Guess: Have an object on a tray, under a cloth covering. Let the children take turns to feel the object without seeing it and guess what it is. When the children are mainly getting it right, substitute for a different object and go round again... and so on. Objects could include: a torch, a key ring, an apple, a safe pencil sharpener, a small light bulb, a comb.

- Circle Time discussion:
  (i) Pets: This would be a good opportunity to ask the children about their pets. What are they? What are they called? (Children who do not have a pet could say what pet they would like to have.) Discuss how they look after their pets. How should we treat creatures? (kindly, gently, with caution, etc.).
  (ii) The senses: Explain that we learn about the world through our senses. Without our sight we would rely more on our other senses – such as hearing.

  Ask the children to tell you about a favourite place (e.g. the seaside; their room; the woods; an adventure playground; their gran's house, etc.).

Awareness activities

- Descriptions: The children should write a description of the place they talked about in the Circle Time discussion using mainly what they see (colour and shapes) with some of what they hear, smell, feel. For example: in the woods they might see tall trees, orange and yellow and red leaves, long, waving green grasses. They might hear birds singing, wind rustling, a stream splashing. They might smell flowers and feel the breeze on their faces etc. Descriptions, of course, always use the senses. It is the senses that reveal the world.

After this, they would write a description of a second place but without the use of 'sight' description. They describe a place they cannot see, increasing what they hear, smell and feel.

- Helping: Ask the children to imagine that Tom has joined their class for a day. What could they do to help him to feel at home? e.g. Ask him about Scamp and talk about their pets; ask him to play the drums for them.
  (i) What could they do to help him? e.g. Show him where things are: the coat pegs, the different areas of the classroom, the toilets, the doorways. How would they guide him? e.g. a light touch on his arm.
  (ii) What should they not do? e.g. Take him somewhere without being sure that is where he wants to go; not tell him when they reach steps, etc.

- Direct experience: The children could take it in turns to wear a blindfold and find their way around the classroom with the help of a friend.

- Visiting speaker: Perhaps you could invite someone from Guide Dogs for the Blind to come to talk about the work of the organisation. Perhaps organise a fund-raising event towards funding the training of a puppy. Alternatively perhaps a member of staff from a school for the blind might come to talk about how to be helpful to blind people and what not to do.

Fun things to make or do

- Sound poem with illustrations: The children could write a poem called 'Sounds I Like'. They can illustrate their poem with lots of small pictures round the edge of the page, showing the sounds being described, e.g. rain on water, etc.

- Good day in Braille: Each child will need a piece of card and a small ball of BluTack. Write 'Good Day' on the blackboard in 'Braille'. (See the Braille alphabet on page 28.) The children can roll small balls of BluTack and stick these on their sheet to make a real (raised) Braille word.

- Stories and pictures: The children could write their own story about a blind boy or girl having an adventure. They could draw or paint a scene from their story or a scene from 'Tom's Famous Bridge', e.g. Tom on his drums, Tom and Mum with Scamp at the stream, Tom or Scamp lost in the thunderstorm, finding Scamp under the bridge.

Co-operative poster

- Make a farm poster: Each child could choose a farm animal to draw, colour and cut out with safety scissors (cow, sheep, horse, duck, pig, etc). Have a poster-sized paper mainly coloured green, divided into fields – perhaps with a blue pond in one corner. The children could stick their creatures in the right place, i.e. the sheep field or the pig pen or the pond.

OR

- A good environment: More ambitiously, older primary school children could make a poster of a 'Good Village' (i.e. good for residents who are blind or partially sighted), e.g. the road crossing lights bleep (some lights now have a vibrating button to let deaf/blind people know when it is safe to cross); the village pond is fenced off; the steps to the building have white edges to guide the partially sighted; there is a Braille map in the centre, etc. Perhaps there is a bandstand in the park. Perhaps you can 'see' into the library and see that Braille and large-print books are available. You will need to decide what the poster will contain and perhaps divide the children into pairs to work on particular sections.

OR

- A welcome poster in Braille: Give each child a photocopy of page 28. The children practise writing 'WELCOME' in Braille following the alphabet guide on their photocopied sheet.

  Next, the children colour and cut up cardboard egg-boxes. Together they stick these on a poster-size sheet to make a welcome poster in Braille.

The Braille alphabet

The Braille alphabet uses a system of raised dots that the reader can feel with his or her finger tips. On this diagram you can see that all the letters are made up from six dots. The black dots would be raised.

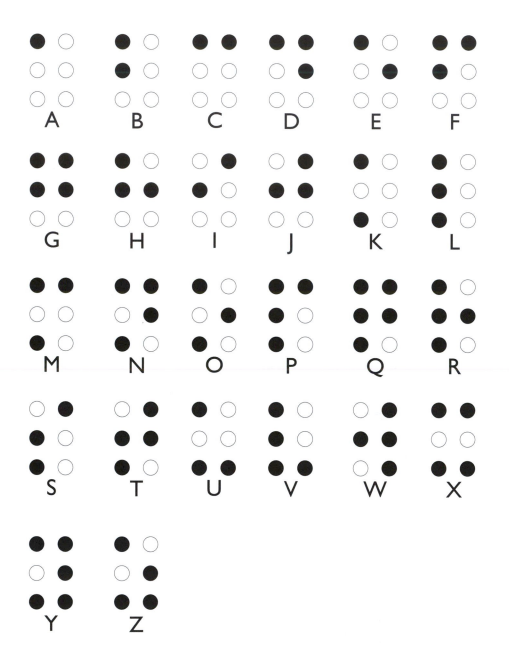

Try your own writing in Braille!

2

The Magic Shoe Box

Background notes

The child in the story

Ellie is eight years old. She had a brain tumour when she was a baby. Ellie nearly died but she was very strong and came through. She had to learn everything all over again. She was very determined and learned most things. Unfortunately, her illness left her with a co-ordination problem and she cannot learn to tie shoelaces or knots.

Ellie has mild learning difficulties but on the whole she copes well at her ordinary school. Her brain damage, when combined with anxiety, however, gives her severe headaches. Ellie lives with her mum and spends time with her dad at weekends.

Ellie is a kind girl with a good best friend in Megan. When she leaves school she wants to work with animals.

Additional points

- Ellie is young for her age and still believes in magic. Some of the younger children who listen to the story will also believe in magic, and some of the older ones will understand that 'The Magic Shoe Box' is just an imaginative name for the shop in the story.

- The story is loosely based on my daughter's experiences with shoes – one of these experiences is mentioned in her own words in Appendix One. Most primary schools are sensible about dress, but in a few, inflexible or insensitive 'rules' still cause problems for some children.

Awareness issues implicit in the story

1. Problems with shoes

Ellie was embarrassed about not being able to tie her shoelaces and her teacher did not realise that Ellie could not do this. Some disabled children also find the encasement of leather shoes to be uncomfortable on sensitive or differently shaped feet. A proportion of the general population have one foot a full size bigger than the other. The imposition of school uniform should take difference/special needs into account – offering flexibility and sensitivity. However, disabled children who 'look' different are sometimes bullied/name-called. Try to be sensitive to a child's wish to 'fit in'.

2. Pain

Ellie suffered from headaches which were made worse by anxiety. Some conditions bring built-in pain, discomfort and tiredness. Professionals need to be aware of this. A school, for example, could have a designated rest room. Stress and anxiety often increase the severity and frequency of pain, and sap energy and efficient learning.

3. Hiding disability

It is sad that many disabled children try to hide or minimise their impairment. An impairment is not something that they should need to feel ashamed of, or embarrassed by. (That they do is a reflection on the social attitudes and values and reactions which they encounter.) Encourage the development of self-esteem and appropriate assertiveness. Ellie had been hiding her inability to tie shoelaces but at the end of the story she decides, very bravely, to defend her new shoes because they match her own needs.

4. Trust and naïvety

Unsurprisingly, parents of disabled children are often protective of their (extra-vulnerable) children. They often have a very close relationship. One consequence is that some disabled children live relatively sheltered lives, and may be particularly trusting and rather naïve. Again, professionals should be sensitive to this. Such children benefit from, and care about, special friends. Their non-disabled friends are often kind and understanding children.

5. Labels can be simplistic

We need to label things – even people. Our use of language depends on categorisation. However, we need to be aware that the labels for disabilities are often clumsy. Like Ellie, a child with learning difficulties may also have a co-ordination problem which is masked by the 'MLD' (mild learning difficulty) label. Children's conditions, their ability and disability profiles do not neatly conform to our labels. Each individual, including his or her impairments and strengths, his or her ability and disability, is unique.

6. Learning difficulty

We should distinguish between a 'learning difficulty' and a 'learning difference'. If learning (in general or in particular areas) is difficult to achieve, this is 'learning difficulty'. Brain-damaged children, such as Ellie, often have some mild, moderate or severe learning difficulty. A 'learning difference' implies not that learning is difficult, but that the process and outcomes may be different from the norm – as for the child with Asperger's syndrome in Chapter 6.

All children learn better at some times that at others, and in some areas more easily than in others. All primary children have some experience of frustration and failure. Very young (pre-school) children do not have the concept of 'failure', and are not deterred. Think how often a toddler falls over before he or she learns to walk. Children with learning difficulties will experience more frustration than the norm. They have to summon extra reserves of determination. It is important that they do not internalise 'failure' and thus damage their self-esteem. Praise and encouragement are important. Measure their progress against what they could not do before, rather than against what most other children can do at their age.

Further reading

Biggs, V. (2005) *Caged in Chaos: A Dyspraxic Guide to Breaking Free.* London: Jessica Kingsley Publishers.

Caldwell, P. (2005) *Finding You Finding Me: Using intensive interaction to get in touch with people whose severe learning disabilities are combined with autistic spectrum disorder.* London: Jessica Kingsley Publishers.

Fairbairn, G. and Fairbairn, S. (1992) *Integrating Special Children: Some Ethical Issues.* London: Avebury.

Storytelling notes

Using the story

As the storyteller, it's likely that you will instinctively structure the timing of the story to provide the children with interesting activities, and will thereby offer them opportunities for stimulation and learning. The plan below is a guide to using the story in an active way, and need not be followed in exactly the sequence that follows – be as creative and flexible with the activities as you like.

Story themes

There are several themes in the story: you could focus on learning profiles (what are you good at and less good at?); magic; friendship; clothes/shoes; dreams; pain and illness.

1. *Introduce the story and theme.* The story is about Ellie who had a serious illness as a child. Ellie is a brave girl, with headaches and worries to cope with. In the story, one problem is solved – in a shoe shop owned by a magician!

2. *Vocabulary.* Make sure the children understand the words. Introduce some of these as they colour the picture, and introduce some in the context – as you come to them in the story.

3. *The story.* Show the illustration and tell or read the story.

4. *Talking about the story.* Use some of the questions and discussion points given, and some of your own, to stimulate the children to talk about the story.

5. *Fun activities for active learning.* The activities include Circle Time games and discussion; things to make, including a co-operative poster for everyone to make together; and 'awareness' activities.

Introduce the story and theme

The story is about Ellie. It is not her fault that she has difficulty with shoes and shoelaces and yet she is made to worry about it. Her shoes become a problem.

Vocabulary

You can introduce some vocabulary as the children colour in the relevant picture, e.g. stripy, trainers, fastened, laces, shoe box, lace-ups, lace-holes, tie, size, slip-ons, undone, court shoes, pumps, leather, decorative, comfortable. (Pictures can be found in Appendix Two.)

Use your usual ways of introducing new words.

minded – cared about

brain tumour – growth inside the head causing illness

co-ordination – matching things, including your movements, together neatly

springy – bouncy

magic – marvellous result using mysterious power

proper – correct

jeering – mocking

tinkled – light, musical sound of a bell

cosy – homely, small and comfortable and warm

moustache – hair over your lip

suspense – excited uncertainty

frown – wrinkle brow/forehead in worry

The story: The Magic Shoe Box

The stripy blue trainers had three straps which pulled over Ellie's foot and fastened with a strong kiss of Velcro. Ellie attached each one with care and sat back, pleased.

'These are cool,' she said, using Megan's favourite word.

'We'll take them,' Mum said to the shop lady. 'We have a problem finding shoes.'

Ellie froze. Surely Mum wouldn't tell?

'Her feet are slightly different sizes you see,' Mum said and Ellie let out her breath in relief.

Thank goodness Mum hadn't mentioned her shoelaces problem. Of all the things that she couldn't do as well as her friends at school, tying her laces was the one she minded most. *Even the babies in Miss Gaynor's class can tie their own shoes*, she thought. Of course she knew it wasn't her own fault. Mum had explained about that.

'The brain tumour you had when you were only a baby left you with a co-ordination problem,' she had said.

All the same, Ellie kept her problem with laces a secret, even from her best friend, Megan.

'Shall I put the trainers in a box for you dear?' said the shopkeeper.

'Can I keep them on, Mum?' Ellie said.

'Sure,' said Mum. She held up the old black leather slip-on shoes. 'These have had it anyway, love.'

On the way out, Mum dropped them in the bin.

Mum and Ellie walked to the bus stop. The trainers felt springy, like walking on soft grass. Across the road from the stop Ellie noticed a small shop called 'The Magic Shoe Box'. It made her think of the song on her Mum's big old record. It was about a girl who wanted magic shoes that would dance all her cares away. It was a song they both liked.

★   ★   ★

The next day Ellie walked proudly to school in her new trainers.

'I like those,' Megan whispered. 'Cool.'

The two friends had desks side by side at the back.

'Stop talking, you two,' said Miss Tight. 'Bring out your books if you've finished. Everyone else has.'

Ellie followed Megan to the front of the class. She always let Megan go first. She was a bit frightened of Miss Tight and scared stiff when she was cross.

Miss Tight noticed her new shoes.

'Those aren't suitable for school,' she said, her voice cold.

Ellie took a deep breath.

'They didn't have black, Miss.' Her voice came out in a whisper.

'The school uniform requires black or dark blue lace-ups,' said Miss Tight. 'Report to me in proper shoes, please. On Monday.' She used her quiet-shout voice and Ellie shivered.

'Tight old moaner,' Megan whispered when they were back at their desks.

Ellie nodded. She felt her eyebrows clench into the frown that gave her headaches. She tried to smooth it away but it kept coming back.

That night Ellie couldn't get to sleep. She tossed and turned, worrying about going to school on Monday. When, eventually, she did fall asleep, she had bad dreams. She dreamed she was at school and had lost one of her shoes.

She was walking down the corridor with only one shoe on and the other kids were pointing and jeering.

The next morning Mum could tell something was wrong.

'Don't you feel well, love?' she asked.

'I've got a headache,' Ellie said.

Mum gave her two of the special headache tablets.

'Are you worried about something?'

'It's my trainers. Miss Tight said I have to wear black lace-ups on Monday.'

'We could buy some today,' Mum said.

'But suppose they come undone at school. What then?'

'I could have a private word with Miss Tight, love, if you like. Surely she could just quietly tie them?'

'No, Mum, please!' said Ellie. 'And what about after PE?'

The children had to change into pumps for PE. Ellie had slip-on pumps, but who would tie her shoes again after the lesson? 'If I leave them undone someone might notice. Or I might trip up,' she said.

'OK,' said Mum. 'We could buy some black leather court shoes. Slip-ons like before. Miss Tight never complained about those.'

'She never noticed, that's all,' said Ellie.

'Well, slip-ons or not?' said Mum. She sounded a bit impatient.

Ellie nodded, but she was anxious. On Monday, when Miss Tight checked her shoes, wouldn't she notice, now, if there were no laces? She seemed to mind about the laces. *If only there were lace-up shoes that never came undone!* thought Ellie. An image of 'The Magic Shoe Box' shop came into her mind. *Could it really be magic?*

'Mum, can we try that shop near the bus stop?' she said.

⋆   ⋆   ⋆

Mum and Ellie opened the door to 'The Magic Shoe Box' and a bell tinkled. It was a small shop. The dark red walls were almost covered up by rows of shoe boxes on shelves. A smiling man came towards them.

'Welcome ladies,' he said. 'Welcome to my Magic Shoe Box. Do come and sit down.'

The man had a huge moustache which curled up at the ends. It was jet black, though his wild curly hair was pure white. *He looks like a magician*, Ellie thought.

'What can I do you for today?' the man said, rubbing his hands and beaming. He looked so friendly that Ellie found herself saying, 'Do you really have magic shoes here?'

'Well,' said the man, winking at Mum, 'what kind of magic did Madam have in mind?'

'Well,' said Ellie, 'lace-up shoes that never come undone.'

'Like a magic purse that you can never empty,' said the man.

Ellie nodded eagerly.

'You'd like one of those I'll bet,' he said to Mum, and he roared with laughter.

'Hang on, though,' he said. 'By jingo, I do believe we might… what size?'

'Threes,' said Mum and Ellie together.

The man hurried off to check his stock in the back of the shop. Ellie could hardly bear the suspense. After a long few minutes the man came back. He had a pair of shoes held high on the flat of his hand.

'Take off your shoes,' he said to Ellie.

He bent down with the ones he had carried in. They slid smoothly onto Ellie's feet.

'Abracadabra!' he shouted. 'Lace-up shoes that never come undone!'

He was smiling broadly.

'Those bows are purely decorative,' he said to Mum.

The magician and Mum were both smiling now.

'Walk round, Ellie,' said Mum.

The magic shoes were very comfortable. Ellie felt her frown smooth away.

Later, however, she began to worry again. Would Miss Tight realise that her shoes were not real lace-ups? She had another restless night. This time she dreamed she was in a big shoe house. It was raining. The rain began to gush through the lace-holes onto her head, like six cold showers. The shoe began to fill with swirling brown water. Ellie was frightened. She was relieved to wake up before the water rose over her head but almost immediately she remembered about Miss Tight and the shoes and her headache came back.

On Monday morning Ellie walked to school feeling very nervous. She hoped Miss Tight would have forgotten but, if not, Ellie had made up her mind to stand up for herself.

'Ellie, let me see your shoes please,' the teacher said, even before they began their work. Ellie walked to the front, her heart thudding. Miss Tight looked down at Ellie's shiny black shoes.

'Are they lace-ups?' she said.

Ellie trembled, but she forced herself to look up at the teacher. Their eyes locked.

'They have laces and are easy to put on, Miss, like I need.' Though Ellie's voice was shaky she spoke up and sounded very determined.

Miss Tight gave her a sharp look. There was a long pause.

'Very smart, dear,' said the teacher, at last. 'Most suitable.'

Ellie walked back to her seat. The magic shoes felt even more springy than her new trainers – like she was walking on air.

Talking about the story

Did the children understand:

- why Ellie liked shoes that fastened with Velcro?

- why Miss Tight did not like Ellie's trainers?

- why Ellie had headaches and bad dreams?

- what Ellie thought the Magic Shoe Box man looked like?

- what Miss Tight said about Ellie's Magic Shoe Box shoes?

Points for discussion

- What is the story about? (e.g. shoes, magic, standing up for yourself, dreams... etc. The children should understand that there is not just one right answer.)

- Do any of the children have a problem with any items of clothing?

- Is your appearance important? (Yes. However, perhaps we can be too concerned...)

- Is your character important? (Yes. It is who you are!)

- What do you like about your own appearance? Your friend's appearance? Your character? Your friend's character? (Use this discussion to bolster self-esteem and to convey that we don't all need to look the same, but we should all try to be kind.)

- We all learn differently. What are you good at learning? What do you find more difficult? Children show determination when they carry on learning even when they find it hard. Why did Ellie have to learn some things many times? (Because she had some learning difficulties from her illness.) Why did Ellie have a co-ordination problem?

Resources

The children could look through their books, or through a story, or a poetry or song anthology to find other relevant stories, poems, rhymes, songs. (They could be about shoes, school, magic, a magician, etc.)

STORIES

Leicester, M. (2004) 'Tales from the Beach.' In *Stories for Inclusive Schools: Developing Young Pupils' Skills*. London: Routledge/Falmer. Another story about a girl who had learning difficulties as a result of a brain tumour.

McCullagh, S. The Puddle Lane Reading Programme. London: Ladybird Books. The Gruffle lived in the Magician's garden. There are several stories about them in this programme.

POEMS

Ahlberg, A. (1984) 'Headmaster's Hymn.' In *Please Mrs Butler*. London: Puffin Books.

Bradman, T. (1989) 'Boots.' In *Smile Please*. London: Puffin Books.

Thurman, J. (1976) 'Going Barefoot.' In J. Foster (ed.) *A First Poetry Book*. Oxford: OUP.

Younger children may like to learn this traditional rhyme:

Cobbler, cobbler mend my shoe,
Get it done by half-past two;
Half-past two is much too late,
Get it done by half-past eight.

Fun activities for active learning

Circle Time

- Circle Time game:
  (i) Good friends: Ask the children to pass this sentence round the circle: 'Good friends…' and they finish the sentence, e.g. Good friends share; Good friend play with you; Good friends laugh at your jokes, etc.

(ii) Kind deeds. Go round the circle for examples of kind deeds. What kind deed could they do today?

- Circle Time discussion:

(i) Friendship: This would be a good opportunity to talk about friendship. What does a good friend do? What is a bad friend like? How can we make new friends? How can we make up when we have quarrelled with our friend? How can we make a new girl or boy in our class feel welcome?

(ii) Compliments and kindness: We all like praise. We like our good points of appearance and character to be noticed and compliments to be made – not comments on our bad points. Kind people praise and pay compliments. Encourage the children to talk about how they feel when people made good and bad comments about them. Go round the circle asking the children to say one good thing about someone else.

Finish by going round the circle saying one good thing about each child. Some children may have a friendly smile or a happy laugh or are often helpful or good at painting, etc. It is particularly important that 'different' children receive a warm (but genuine) compliment. (When praising children's work or behaviour try to make your praise as specific as you can. For example, 'You have worked hard,' rather than, 'You have been good,' so that they understand exactly what you are approving.)

Awareness activities

- Poems: Tell the children Ellie has poor co-ordination and learning difficulties about number. Discuss why Ellie found these difficult and why she was embarrassed. Ask what the children find difficult and what they are good at and emphasise that the important thing is to try. Ellie is very good with words. She wrote these 'recipe' poems.

  A Good Friend
  Take a teaspoon of smiles
  A tablespoon of fun
  A cupful of sharing
  For one good friend

A Kindness
Take a teaspoon of understanding
A tablespoon of smiles
A cupful of helping
For one kind deed

The children can write their own 'recipe' poems.

- Staring: Explain to the children that Ellie has a scar at the back of her head, from when she had her illness and had an operation. She hated people staring at this. She wrote this poem:

Staring
You know it's bad manners,
The rudest you can be,
Everyone is told it,
So why stare at me?
Surely you know better
Surely you can see
Staring is very mean
So why stare at me?

Discuss why people stare and with the children's help make a list of reasons, e.g. people are interested and don't realise they are staring; they are being mean – a kind of bullying; they don't know it is bad manners.

Fun things to make or do

- Differences: A portrait: Ellie was self-conscious about her scar. Other people might be self-conscious about other aspects of their appearance. What else? (Get the children to make suggestions, e.g. wearing glasses, being very tall, short, thin, overweight or in a wheelchair, wearing a hearing aid, having different kind of clothes.)

    Think what a boring world it would be if we were all the same!

    Let the children draw a positive portrait of a 'pretend' friend who looks different in some way, e.g. a girl with really cool glasses; a short boy with a cool haircut and cool clothes (perhaps he has a football at his feet because he is good at football); a sweet friendly alien; a boy in a stylish cool, 'racer' looking wheelchair; a pretty plump girl with long blonde hair and a lovely smile.

- Differences: A poem: Reiterate the point about how boring things would be if we were all the same. Talk about cultural differences in dress, food, art and music and show some positive pictures, e.g. someone wearing a beautiful sari, a 'helping' person in a uniform (e.g. a nurse). Talk about how we all have different interests. What are their interests? What are the interests and hobbies of their family members? Let them write a poem celebrating differences: 'Our Interesting World'.

- Differences: A story: Each child could select one of the 'pretend' friends from the portraits. (They can choose their own if they wish or use one of the illustrations in this book.) They could write a story in which this person is a hero or heroine in some way.

Co-operative poster

- A frieze: Let the children stick their portraits on a long sheet of paper to make a 'different friends' frieze along one wall.

OR

- A different-dress poster: If you have a large number of unwanted magazines let the children find examples of different kinds of dresses from different cultures; different uniforms; different occasions – sport, holidays, ball gowns, weddings. Using safe scissors they cut these out and stick them on to a large poster-size sheet. If there are lots of gaps on the poster, the children could draw some 'different' people in 'different' dress, uniforms and costumes.

3

A Kind Revenge

Background notes

The child in the story

When Jack was born, one of his legs was shorter than the other, and very twisted. He learned to walk with sticks. He was always brave about going into hospital and having operations to straighten his leg.

Jack gets depressed that he can't join in such things as running. However, he is generous in his support of his friend Dan, whenever Dan races, and proud of his friend.

Jack lives with his dad.

Additional points

- Jack takes a mild revenge against the boy who bullies him, Becks, by directing one of his jokes against him. At a deeper level, he is attracted to comedy and to 'alternative' comedy because it is a socially acceptable way of getting his own back against bullies and their prejudiced attitudes!

- The verbal abuse in the story was originally strong and more offensive. I had heard children called 'crippo'! I decided to tone reality down! However, you can change the language to be appropriate for the children you are telling the story to, for example by substituting 'jerk' for 'crip'. The issue of *bad* 'name-calling', however, is an important one for children who look different. It is an aspect of bullying which happens frequently and which needs to be addressed.

- Sadly, many children (disabled *and* non-disabled) experience a substantial degree of bullying.

Awareness issues implicit in the story

1. Name-calling and bullying

Many non-disabled children experience name-calling and bullying. Disabled children, particularly in mainstream schools, may be particularly vulnerable. It is very important that all professionals, parents and organisations seek to establish a non-bullying culture in their children's world. Your own example of non-bullying is important – as is how you deal with bullying: taking it seriously and having a consistent policy about it, for example. Adults need to be sensitive to children's experiences of bullying. The children, too, need to learn that it is wrong, and what to do about it. Relevant activities are given at the end of this chapter.

As children and even as adults we are all potential victims of bullying. (The incidence of bullying at work is surprisingly high.) The perception of someone as 'different' is often the trigger for bullying behaviour. A good education teaches children to be interested rather than threatened by 'difference'. If children unlearn social prejudices against social minorities this will tend to reduce bullying.

2. 'Minor' impairment

Children who are doing well at mainstream school and coping well with a relatively minor impairment may, paradoxically, be particularly targeted for bullying and particularly liable to internalise their own unfavourable judgement on their deviation from the mythical 'norm'. Be sensitive to their emotional needs.

3. Pushing oneself

All children reach their fullest potential when they have pushed themselves in their learning and achievements. With disabled children it would be wrong not to recognise extra difficulties and the extra effort and energy that are required, making due allowances. However, it would also be wrong not to encourage them to try their best. It is easy to expect too little. Low expectations can be self-fulfilling. Let a child's interests and inclinations lead – but follow with advice, praise, encouragement, reward and support. (Not all children would be as willing to put themselves on the spot and in the spotlight as much as Jack.)

4. Self-esteem

It is important to build up children's self-esteem. Help them to like themselves by helping them to accept their strengths and weaknesses. It will add to their self-esteem if they see that you like them. Try to increase their self-reliance, self-expression and self-confidence, along with their social skills. Like Jack's teacher in the story, find something each child is good at.

Further reading

Baker, K. and Smith, B. (2006) *Making a Spectacle of Bullying*. London: Sage.

Dubin, N. (2006) *Being Bullied: Strategies and Solutions for People with Asperger's Syndrome*. London: Jessica Kingsley Publishers.

Horwath, J. (ed.) (2001) *The Child's World: Assessing Children in Need*. London: Jessica Kingsley Publishers.

Rigby, K. (2002) *Stop the Bullying: A Handbook for Schools*. London: Jessica Kingsley Publishers.

Storytelling notes

Using the story

As the storyteller, it's likely that you will instinctively structure the timing of the story to provide the children with interesting activities, and will thereby offer them opportunities for stimulation and learning. The plan below is a guide to using the story in an active way, and need not be followed in exactly the sequence that follows – be as creative and flexible with the activities as you like.

Story themes

There are several themes in the story you could focus on, such us name-calling/bullying, humour or using your talents and skills.

1. *Introduce the story and theme.* This story is about Jack who gets called names by a boy at school. Jack finds something he likes and is good at, and in so doing takes a gentle revenge on the boy who bullied him.

2. *Vocabulary.* Make sure the children understand the words. Introduce some of these as they colour the picture, and introduce some in the context – as you come to them in the story.

3. *The story.* Show the illustration and tell or read the story.

4. *Talking about the story.* Use some of the questions and discussion points given, and some of your own, to stimulate the children to talk about the story.

5. *Fun activities for active learning.* The activities include Circle Time games and discussion, things to make, including a co-operative poster for everyone to make together, and 'awareness' activities.

Introduce the story and theme

- The story is about Jack. He gets picked on by another boy who calls him names. Name-calling is a form of bullying and bullying is wrong.

- Jack discovers he is good at telling jokes. Do the children know what 'alternative' comedy means: that it is comedy with a message; that makes jokes *against* bad, bullying attitudes and social prejudices? This is the kind of comedian Jack wants to be.

Vocabulary

You can introduce some vocabulary as the children colour in the relevant picture, e.g. walk with sticks, sports day, starting line, finishing line, thumbs up, punched the air. (Pictures can be found in Appendix Two.)

don't bother – don't trouble

bunch – in a group

aggressively – threateningly

a spurt of – a jet of

snarl – a fierce look

encounter – meeting

stand-up – a comedian who tells jokes one after the other

guts – courage

variety show – with different kinds of acts (singers, dancers, comedians, etc.)

weaving – threading

pinched – stole

favourite jokes – the jokes they liked best

'dried up' – forgot his lines/jokes

scared – frightened

(negative) prejudice – unfair, biased ideas and feelings

The story: A Kind Revenge

'More toast, Jack?' said Dad.

I shook my head.

'What is it, son?'

He put a hand on my shoulder and I swallowed hard.

'Nothing, Dad. Really. Honest.'

'But, nothing really what… ?'

'Oh, I'm just feeling sorry for myself, that's all. Sports day and that.'

'I'd forgotten! Sorry.' Dad knows I hate feeling left out and useless.

'Well, why should you remember? I said. 'I told you not to come in any case.'

'You don't need to go either. I'll send a note if you like. Saying you're not feeling too good.'

I hesitated. It was tempting. I'd never told Dad about Becks. He picks on me when he gets a chance and on sports day there would be less adults watching him. I was a bit worried, but I wanted to be there for Dan.

'No. I have to go. For Dan,' I said. 'His parents can't be there, see.'

I collected my sticks and set off. In fact, once at school, even though I couldn't join in myself, watching Dan go to the starting line, I felt much better. He's really good. He saw me and raised a hand, grinning.

The whistle blew and they were off, about 20 runners in a bunch. Very soon Dan and another boy drew ahead. Like raindrops on a window they ran faster and faster, but exactly together. I cheered Dan like mad. They were in sight of the finishing line when Dan made a great effort and pulled ahead to cross first. He bent over to catch his breath, straightened and gave me a thumbs up. I grinned and punched the air.

'What you so pleased about, Jack-In-A-Box?' someone said.

It was Becks. He calls me Jack-In-A-Box because of my up-and-down walk and one or two of his mates have started to pick it up too. I hate it.

'I asked you a question, jerk-along. You deaf as well?'

Becks stuck his head forward aggressively.

'My mate won,' I muttered.

'Yeah, well, you'll never win any prizes, crip, that's for sure,' he said, and he laughed.

Several kids were listening now and a spurt of anger made me stand up to him.

'Whereas you could take gold for being mean,' I said.

One or two of the kids laughed and I grinned. Becks moved towards me, his face in a snarl, but one of the other kids was his football team captain.

'Leave it, Becks,' he said.

★   ★   ★

All day I kept hearing Beck's words in my mind.

'You'll never win any prizes.'

It hurt. It wasn't just sport I couldn't do. I wasn't particularly good at anything. I never came near the top of the class. Not like Dan.

At home-time my teacher took me to one side.

'A little bird told me about your encounter with Becks.' She smiled her nice smile. 'You want me to speak to him about his horrid four-letter word?'

I shook my head, grinning.

'He's a four-letter word himself,' I said, and she laughed.

'You're good at making people laugh, Jack. Why not do a stand-up in the show?'

I stared at her, struck by the idea. *Well, I'm not good at much else*, I thought.

'It takes guts to do stand-up.'

'Yeah,' I said. 'Case no-one laughs.'

She nodded. 'Exactly.'

We were quiet for a moment.

'Think about it,' she said.

★   ★   ★

The next school 'play', for the first time ever, was to be a variety show. Everyone was excited about it, talking about who could do what. Dan was thinking of playing his guitar. I don't play an instrument or sing or anything and sort of thought there was nothing I could do. I felt left out and useless again. But now I began to study the comedians on the telly. It was really interesting. There's more to it than you'd think. It's not just having good jokes. It's how you tell them, like weaving them into a story, or one coming out of another. Even the pauses matter, and the faces they make.

I noticed that different comedians have different kinds of jokes. I pinched some of the best ones. And I began to ask all my friends and relatives for their favourites, and pinched a few of those too.

After that, I decided how to weave my jokes into an act, and I told my teacher I would do it in the show. Later I got scared and thought of pulling out, but by then it was too late. I'd been put in the programme.

★   ★   ★

The big evening arrived. I was really scared now. I wished I hadn't said I'd do it. Dad with a whole row of our relatives would be there! Suppose I dried up, forgot my lines. Suppose no one laughed, and Becks and his mates jeered at me after.

By the time I was waiting in the wings for my turn I was terrified. I was on after Dan's guitar spot, just before the interval. Dan played really well – three pieces. Everyone clapped very loud and he came off grinning.

'Good luck, Jack,' he whispered, and I was on.

The hall was packed. Row upon row of people watched as I heaved myself to the centre of the stage, my sticks loud on the boards. I faced the upturned faces and the staring eyes. Becks was right on the front with his mates. They waited. There were a few coughs and rustles and then, silence. I delivered my opening stiffly. My voice sounded nervous, even to me.

'What's brown and sticky?' I said, and I answered too quickly. 'A stick of course!'

There was only a small spatter of laughter and above this Becks did a loud groan. I felt like walking off, a complete fool.

'This is going to be a disaster,' I said, 'unless we loosen up.'

It just came out. It wasn't in my script and it wasn't meant to be a joke, but they laughed – real laughter – and I relaxed. I felt they were with me. I sounded more confident in the next joke – about a footballer who's a bit of a bully and comes unstuck! They knew who I meant, that's for sure. The kids roared with laughter. I loved that. After that, I couldn't go wrong! I told a few of my favourite jokes and the whole audience laughed every time – louder and louder. I finished with a couple of great jokes, which were kind of sticking up for disabled people. It cracked them up.

It was a great feeling. I could make them laugh at their own daft prejudice! I loved every minute. Each roar of delicious laughter filled me with pleasure. I feasted on it. This was something I was good at!

At the end, full to bursting, I gave a little bow and applause thundered out. It followed me as I left the stage, drowning out the sound of my sticks, and I knew that I wanted to do this for ever.

Talking about the story

Did the children understand:

- why Jack felt sorry for himself?
- why Jack needed to go to school to support his friend Dan?
- why it was brave to do the 'stand-up' for the variety show?
- why the story is called 'A Kind Revenge'?

Points for discussion

- What is the story about? (e.g. name-calling, bullying, telling jokes, turning the tables on someone, etc. The children should understand that there is not just one right answer.)

- Would Jack's dad have been telling a lie if he had sent the note saying Jack wasn't well? (Jack was feeling depressed; you could also introduce the concept of a 'white' lie. How is a white lie different from other lies? Is it still wrong?)

- Was Jack's teacher a good teacher? (The children should give reasons for their answer.)

- Discuss humour and laughter. (Why do we like to laugh? What kinds of things make us laugh? Why did Jack enjoy making people laugh?)

Resources

The children could look through their books, or through a story, or poem or song anthology to find other relevant stories, poems, rhymes, songs. They could be about name-calling, bullying, humour, shows, sports or sports day, etc.

STORIES

Andersson, S. (1980) *No Two Zebras are the Same.* London: Lion Publications.

Leicester, M. (2004) *Stories for Inclusive Schools: Developing Young Pupils' Skills.* London: Routledge/Falmer.

POEMS

Bradman, T. (1989) 'The Name Game.' In *Smile Please.* London: Puffin Books.

Goldthorpe, M. (2001) 'Who's a Bully?' In *Poems for Circle Time and Literacy Hour.* Wisbech: LDA. Contains other useful poems and material relevant to bullying.

Fun activities for active learning

Circle Time

- Circle Time game:
  (i) Names: Ask the children to think of a name they like. Go round the circle. Each child says the name they chose.
  (ii) Jokes: Ask the children to think of a joke they like. Let the children tell their joke.

- Circle Time discussion:
  (i) Name-calling: Have any of you been bullied? What did you do? How did you feel? You feel bad even though it is not your fault!

How did Becks bully Jack? (Name-calling.) Should we call people names? Why not? What can we do about it? (e.g. ignore it; remind ourselves that the bully is insecure and doing a bad action, and we should try not to let it hurt us.) If the name-calling gets worse or moves on to other forms of bullying (stone throwing, hitting) tell an adult you trust.

(ii) Assertiveness: Jack stood up to Beck's insults. This is good to do when it is safe to do so. (Otherwise you need the help of an understanding adult.)

How can we deal with insults? Examples:

- make a joke

- walk away

- ignore it and carry on with what we are doing.

How can we say 'no' to things we don't want to do? (Let the children try to think what to do in these situations and you can give the following suggestion if they don't.)

- Give me some money! (No, I don't have any. No. I only have my dinner money so the teacher/my mum will find out.)

- Give me those sweets. (Sorry, I licked them already.)

- Do my homework for me. (No. The teacher can tell.)

- Can I borrow your trainers? (No. Your feet are smaller than mine. You'll get blisters.)

- You've pinched my pen. (No, I haven't. Let the teacher check my bag.)

(iii) Self-esteem: Let's remind ourselves of what we are good at. Go round the circle asking the children to say one thing they are good at or a good thing they have done. Go round the circle asking the children to say one thing they like about themselves. (You could give some examples, e.g. I am kind to animals; I am friendly; I help my mum; I like my hair, etc.)

Awareness activities

- Dealing with name-calling: Arrange the children into pairs. Each pair should think of ways they could deal with name-calling. Each pair will tell their ideas and you could make a list. Make sure the list includes: ignore the name-calling as though you don't care; walk away; tell an adult you trust.

- Why do people bully?: Children who pick on other children all the time do it because it makes them feel better. They have a problem. With the children make another list of suggestions of why people might bully others, e.g. they are being bullied themselves, they act 'tough' to avoid being the one to be bullied, they are jealous of the person they bully, they are sad or angry and take this out on someone else. How could they try to change and to stop? (e.g. make friends with non-bullying children, say sorry to someone they have bullied and promise to stop, join a new club for a fresh start.)

  After making the lists explain to the children that bullying is cowardly because the person picks on someone weaker or smaller who can't fight back. They pick on people's differences because they have never understood that we are all different and this makes getting to know people more interesting.

Fun things to make or do

- Telephone advice: In pairs the children can take turns to 'phone' each other with a bullying problem. Someone in their class keeps scribbling on their book or name-calling in the playground or picking on them on the way home. They discuss the problem with their friend on the phone. What can they do about this problem?

  After the activity talk about the ideas they had and comment on the good ones.

  You could give the children the telephone numbers of these free helplines – ChildLine: 0800 1111; Samaritans: 08457 909090.

- Two stories: Jack found a way of dealing with Becks. First he made a joke when Becks was saying unpleasant things and then he poked fun at him (indirectly) in his act. Write two short stories. In one story Jack finds a different way of dealing with Becks. Don't make it too unkind or Jack will be the bully! In the other, Becks changes – he stops being a bully. Write about what happened to make him change into a kinder boy.

- Under the spotlight: Paint a picture with Jack (or your friend, or someone you make up) on the stage in the spotlight. How can you paint the spotlight? Will you paint curtains at the side of the stage?

Co-operative poster

- How to Deal with Bullying chart: Write the best suggestions that arose from the children about dealing with bullies, on a poster-sized sheet. Give each of the children a small square of card. The children can draw and colour something beautiful. (A butterfly or flower or favourite person or favourite food, etc.) Let the children stick the cards round the 'How to Deal with Bullying' chart to form an attractive border or frame. This will be a good poster to have on the wall. It will remind the children of what they can do if they are bullied.

- Saying 'No' poster: Write the best suggestions that arose from the children about how to say 'No' to various demands. Again these could be written on a poster-sized sheet and given a 'frame' or 'border' made by the children.

- Things we are good at: Write the list of things the children have said that they are good at and/or like about themselves. Again the children could decorate the poster with their pasted-on cards of beautiful things.

   NB. You could do all three posters. Place them together and paste the cards round the outer edge of all three.

4

One and One Make Trouble

Background notes

> ### The children in the story
>
> Harry and Connor are twins. They both have attention deficit hyperactivity disorder (ADHD). They are bright boys who share an obsessive interest in numbers. This means that they are very good at mathematics and enjoy number-based games and puzzles on their computers. They live with their mum and dad and older sister, Jessica. The story is partly about Jessica too.

Additional points

- It is important that the children understand that Harry and Connor do not mean to be naughty.

- The children should also be understanding and sympathetic to Mum and Dad and Jessica!

- Many children will have been upset by overhearing parental quarrels and been angry with brothers and sisters. They will readily identify with Jessica's feelings.

Awareness issues implicit in the story

1. A mix of conditions

As with any 'disabling' condition, children with ADHD may have other impairments to cope with too. Multiple conditions may aggravate each other.

What is ADHD? The key triad defining ADHD are inattention, hyperactivity and impulsivity. 'Inattentive' symptoms include: distractibility and organisational difficulties arising from being forgetful ('absent minded'). Symptoms of hyperactivity and impulsivity include: being fidgety, talking excessively, being constantly active ('on-the-go'), interrupting, acting on impulse.

2. 'Difficult' symptoms

The symptoms of this condition interfere with home and school and social life. Because such symptoms are not easy to live with, it is important that we recognise the child has a *neurological condition* which makes it difficult to stay attentive and to control his or her impulses. He or she is not deliberately being naughty, disorganised, irritating or mean!

3. Coping with symptoms

There are strategies which help carers and teachers to cope with children with ADHD. For example:

- Such children can pay attention when they are fascinated by an activity and these interests can be used. (As in the story.) However, try to eliminate potential distractions and present material in an attention-grabbing way.

- Build in opportunity for physical activity – handing out materials, out-of-seat breaks/exercises, etc.

- Make use of notebooks to aid memory and concentration. Use plans to break down tasks and to check on tasks completed and tasks still undone.

4. Siblings

The brothers and sisters of disabled children need our consideration too. We know that having a disabled brother or sister often encourages the development of caring qualities, but we must also be aware that sometimes children may resent the extra attention and time that their sibling's impairment may require. We cannot expect children to be understanding beyond their years. In this story we are reminded that a disabled child's impairments may impact on the whole family.

5. *Good points*

It is important for our own responses (as carers and teachers) and for a child's self-esteem that we remind ourselves of every child's good qualities and of positive aspects of every situation and try to be creative in thinking about ways of supporting children who need additional or different kinds of help. Children with ADHD, for example, are good at living in the present moment; something we get less good at doing as adults. Perhaps we should sometimes be sufficiently flexible to follow the children's unexpected or sudden engagements and enthusiasm and 'go with the flow'. Children with ADHD can be a lot of fun. They are never dull and often creative. As Martin Kutscher says in his recommended book (see Further reading), 'It's going to be quite a ride.'

Further reading

Hames, A. and McCaffrey, M. (eds) (2005) *Special Brothers and Sisters: Stories and Tips for Siblings of Children with a Disability or Serious Illness.* London: Jessica Kingsley Publishers.

Kutscher, M.L. (2005) *Kids in the Syndrome Mix of ADHD, LD, Asperger's, Tourette's, Bipolar, and More! The one stop guide for parents, teachers, and other professionals.* London: Jessica Kingsley Publishers.

Shore, K. (2002) *Special Kids Problem Solver: Ready-to-Use Interventions for Helping all Students with Academic, Behavioural and Physical Problems.* London: Jossey-Bass.

Storytelling notes

Using the story

As the storyteller, it's likely that you will instinctively structure the timing of the story to provide the children with interesting activities, and will thereby offer them opportunities for stimulation and learning. The plan below is a guide to using the story in an active way, and need not be followed in exactly the sequence that follows – be as creative and flexible with the activities as you like.

Story themes

There are several themes in the story: you could focus on ADHD; brothers and sisters; family disagreements, etc.

1. *Introduce the story and theme.* In this story we see how teatime in one family becomes disrupted by the twin brothers' hyperactive

behaviour. They find it difficult to behave differently but their older sister finds a good solution.

2. *Vocabulary.* Make sure the children understand the words. Introduce some of these as they colour the picture, and introduce some in context – as you come to them in the story.

3. *The story.* Show the illustration and tell or read the story.

4. *Talking about the story.* Use some of the questions and discussion points given, and some of your own, to stimulate the children to talk about the story.

5. *Fun activities for active learning.* The activities include Circle Time games and discussion, things to make, including a co-operative poster for everyone to make together, and 'awareness' activities.

Introduce the story and theme

- The twin boys in this story cannot change their behaviour very easily because they have a condition called attention deficit hyperactivity disorder.

- When we *can* behave with more consideration for other people, then of course we should!

- When there is a reason why it is difficult to be more considerate, however, sometimes a helpful solution can be found.

Vocabulary

You can introduce some vocabulary as the children colour in the relevant picture, e.g. favourite, scoff, obsessed, individual things, totals, score. (Pictures can be found in Appendix Two.)

plonked – placed heavily

favourite – the (one) you like best

gloating – exulting over someone else

jiggling – slightly bouncing up and down

bribery – money in exchange for someone doing what you want

crater – open part at the top of a volcano where the lava comes out

patient – keeping calm; not losing your temper

specialist – expert in one subject

interact – relate to each other

weirdest – oddest

attention – giving your consideration and concentration

emphasis – stressing, giving importance to

The story: One and One Make Trouble

Mum plonked two loaded plates, one each, in front of Harry and Connor. She served my brothers first because otherwise they might rush off without eating anything.

'Your favourite,' she said. 'Fish fingers and chips.' They began to scoff their food.

'I've got more than you,' Harry said. He wasn't gloating. They were just obsessed by numbers and immediately began to count their chips.

I would have been told off for not waiting until we were all served, but not the twins! You wouldn't believe what they get away with.

'Fifteen, me,' Harry said.

'You're right then,' said Connor. 'Fourteen, me.'

Mum gave Dad his plate and mine to me. 'Eat up, Jessica,' she said, but the moment Mum sat down with her own tea Harry sprang to his feet, jiggling with excitement. He pointed to the window at the far end of the room. 'Look!' he yelled.

A bird had perched on the window sill outside. Harry ran across to the window and the bird flew away.

'Harry. Come back at once!' Dad said.

'Now look what you've gone and done, Dad. Made it fly away. Shouting!' Harry shouted.

'Sit down.' Dad's voice was quiet but angry. 'That is no way for a seven-year-old to talk to his father.'

'How old would you have to be?' asked Connor. I could tell he was really interested. Numbers again. But Dad heard it as cheek.

'You be quiet too,' he said.

'I was only asking what… '

'I said, "be quiet".' Dad did shout that time.

Connor ran from the room, slamming the door behind him.

Harry sprang up again, knocking over his chair.

'I know,' he yelled. He grabbed a handful of his chips, ran to the window, opened it and scattered them over the sill. He turned back to us.

'The bird might come back for the chips, right?'

Dad gave a huge sigh and Mum put down her knife and fork. She worried that the twins didn't eat enough, but she couldn't eat any more either. Her face was white.

'These meal times are the pits,' Dad said. He glanced at the big clock over the cooker. 'They've ruined this one in less than ten minutes. We really do have to do something.'

* * *

The best time of the day is after the twins have gone to bed. I sit with Mum and Dad and we read or watch the telly. The fire makes small, cosy crackles and the house is incredibly peaceful. That night Dad repeated what he had said at teatime.

'We really have to do something.'

'You know it's their ADHD,' Mum said, her voice sad. 'They can't help it.'

'Well, I can't help getting mad,' said Dad. 'I try to be patient but… ' he shook his head.

'What can we do?' I asked.

'Bribery doesn't work,' said Dad. 'I've tried that.'

'And red doesn't,' I said, and we all laughed.

Red is the twins' favourite colour and Mum once made a red tea: sliced ham, sliced beetroot and mash potato coloured with the beetroot juice. They loved the look of it but they made volcanoes with the mash and got into a furious row with each other when Connor scooped a crater out of Harry's pointed mountain. One plateful ended up smashed on the floor. 'The red potato makes it look as though the white plate is bleeding,' Connor had said.

'We could eat after they're in bed,' I suggested.

Mum shook her head.

'It's so late, Jessica, and too near your bedtime.'

'You and me could,' Dad said to her.

I didn't like that idea, but was too sorry for Mum to say anything.

At bedtime Mum gave me an extra-tight hug. 'Sleep tight, Jess. Try not to worry about it.'

In fact I lay awake for a long time. Mum and Dad were pretty patient with my brothers but teatime stressed them out more than anything.

After a while I got up to go to the loo and I heard Mum and Dad arguing.

'I could just shove the food in their room while they're playing number games on the computer! Would that suit you? Remember the specialist said we're supposed to interact as a family.' There was a wobble of tears in her voice.

'He should try eating with them,' Dad said. 'Look, we could sit with them but still eat our own meal in peace, later, when they're in bed.'

'That's not fair on Jessica. Why should she eat with them and not us?'

'So we all have to suffer. Is that it?'

Dad sounded angry and I crept back to my room feeling bad. Now my parents were actually rowing about teatime. Teatime and me! If only I could think of something we could do – like Dad had said.

When at last I fell asleep I dropped into one unpleasant dream after another. In the weirdest one, all the numbers on our big kitchen clock jumped out and became number people. Number 1 was a tall straight man. Two was a bent old lady. The double numbers, 10, 11 and 12, were made by two people holding hands. My twin brothers were number 11. They began to put the other numbers in the right order – leaving a gap between 10 and 12 for themselves.

'What shall we do with her?' asked number 9, a thin lady with a big, sad face. She was pointing at me.

'She's the spare number 1,' the tall number one said.

'The odd one out,' they all chanted.

I woke up then, feeling sad for a moment, but the sadness whooshed up like a gas fire and flared into excitement.

I know what we can do, I thought. *It just might work!* I went down to breakfast with a scary mixture of hope and worry hidden inside.

Mum was alone in the kitchen. The twins were still upstairs and Dad, as usual, had already gone to work.

'Mum, I've had an idea about what we can do at teatime. It might work!'

Mum looked at me. I could feel a huge grin on my face.

'What?' she said, and I heard the sudden hope in her voice.

'It's a secret until I try it,' I said. 'But will you get me two notebooks and pens?'

'Sure.'

'And please can we have individual things for tea?'

'Individual things? What do you mean, Jess?'

'Chips or new potatoes – not mash. Carrots or sprouts – not cabbage.'

'Sure,' she said again. She sounded more doubtful, the hope gone from her voice.

By teatime I was wound up, almost as fidgety as my brothers. I gave them a notebook each.

'You have to record in your notebook the number of things you eat and the number you leave,' I said. 'You work out the total at the end. Can you eat more than you leave?'

The twins listened to this, their attention caught by the emphasis on numbers. They immediately ate two out of their three fish fingers. They both wrote: 'fish fingers $2 - 1 = 1$'.

They gobbled some of their chips next and wrote: 'chips $10 - 5 = 5$'. Mum and Dad exchanged a smile and Dad winked at me.

'Ugh, carrots,' Harry said.

Connor glanced at his brother's notebook. 'You only need to eat one.'

'And leave five!' said Harry. 'Yeah!'

He ate one, pulling a face.

Connor liked carrots and ate four.

'See if you can catch Connor up at pudding,' Dad said to Harry.

This kept the twins interested in their fruit salad.

'The cream doesn't count,' Mum said.

Connor doesn't like grapes and left all of his with the happy result that their final totals came out the same: '17'.

'Can we do it again tomorrow, Mum?' Harry said.

Mum smiled. 'Yes of course, dear.'

'See who has the highest score by the end of the week,' suggested Dad.

'Me!'

'No, me!'

The twins ran upstairs shouting 'me' all the way up.

'Well done, Jessica,' Dad said. 'That was a brilliant idea. You can have an extra half-hour before bed for every teatime that it works. Fair enough, Mum?'

Mum nodded.

'I bet it'll work 'til they completely fill up their books,' I said.

Mum smiled at me and scraped up the last bit of her fruit salad.

Talking about the story

Did the children understand:

- why teatimes were difficult for the family?

- why Jessica's notebook idea worked for her brothers?

Points for discussion

- What is the story about? (e.g. ADHD, brothers and sisters, quarrelling, dreams, teatime.) The children should understand there is not just one right answer.

- *Responsibility and blame.* Why were Connor and Harry not just very naughty children? (They had ADHD which influenced their behaviour.) When are we to blame for what we do? (When we do it on purpose and could have behaved differently.) Jessica blamed herself for her parents' row, but was she really to blame?

- *Group behaviour.* Connor and Harry's ADHD was hard on the whole family at teatime, until Jessica found a solution. Are there any problems we have in our group/class? (This is an opportunity for the children (and you) to identify problem behaviour of their own or others and for supportive solutions to be found.)

- *Problems with brothers and sisters.* Harry and Connor spoiled teatime for their sister. Do we have any problems with our brothers and sisters? What (fair and sensible) solutions can we think of?

Resources

The children could look through their books, or through a story, or poetry or song anthology, to find other relevant stories, poems, rhymes, songs. (They could be about inattention, quarrels, birds, numbers, dreams, twins, brothers and sisters.)

STORIES

Harper, A. (1987) *The Fighting Sisters*. London: Macdonald.

Hughes, S. (1995) *The Trouble with Jack*. London: Rex Fox.

Leicester, M. (2006) 'The Power of a Smile.' In *Stories for Circle Time and Assembly: Developing Literary Skills and Classroom Values*. London: Routledge/Falmer.

POEMS

Ahlberg, A. (1984) 'Small Quarrel.' In *Please Mrs Butler*. London: Puffin.

Fun activities for active learning

Circle Time

- Favourite food: Go round the circle asking the children to name their favourite food. Now go round and ask what food they most hate.

- Sharing a dream: Jessica had a dream that gave her a good idea. Let the children take turns to tell a dream they have had – pleasant or scary.

- Circle Time discussion: Ask the children to say which good behaviour they find the most difficult to do or remember to do (e.g. not interrupt when someone is speaking; not talk with a mouthful of food; not make too much noise in the classroom or library; not spoil new clothes, etc.). Choose some of these and see if the group can brainstorm some helpful tips for making it easier to do or remember to do the 'good' behaviour.

Awareness activities

- Concentration: Divide the children into small groups. Give each group a list of tasks, e.g. puzzles, sums, spelling list to learn. Each child takes a turn to complete a task on the list while the other (one or two) try to distract them by talking to them, or perhaps even telling jokes.

- Building a tower: Practise co-ordination in a fun activity. Still in their small groups, who can build the highest tower of bricks? (When the tower collapses the next child has a turn.)

- Making up: Jessica was sad to hear her mum and dad quarrelling. We all quarrel with our friends and family from time to time. What can we do to make up? Let the children give suggestions – some perhaps prompted by you. You could write a list of good suggestions, for example:

  ○ I could say sorry.

  ○ I could smile or speak first.

  ○ I could help my friend.

  ○ I could share something with my friend.

  ○ We could talk about why we fell out.

  ○ I could say something nice to my friend.

- Understanding our particular needs: This is an opportunity for the children to share information with each other provided this will lead to an increased understanding. The special needs could be very inclusive, i.e. whatever the children regard as one (e.g. ADHD; poor hearing, illness in the family; wearing glasses; diabetes; poor co-ordination; dyslexia; epilepsy; eczema; asthma). (You will need to explain these conditions to the children, but you can discuss as a group how you could all be helpful in response to each 'need.')

Fun things to make or do

- Notebooks: Give each child a new notebook – their Numbers Notebook. What numbers will they record? It could be, as in the story, the food items they eat and leave at lunchtime. You could take a walk in the school grounds and count the number of flowers, birds, trees, etc. You could look round the room: how many windows, pictures, children? The recorded numbers could then be a useful base for some adding and subtracting, e.g. How much more did you eat than leave? How many more flowers did you see than birds? How many things did you put down altogether?

- An 'interest' project: Give each child a big notebook or file. Like Harry and Connor we all concentrate and learn better when we are very interested in something. Get the children to identify a subject which they find interesting and which could become their learning project. Using visits to the library, group discussion, and appropriate contacts, etc., the children could each build up information and pictures about their chosen subject, to fill their project notebook or file. Later they could give short talks to the group, about their subject.

- The story in pictures: Let the children do small pictures of the various 'scenes' in the story 'One and One Make Trouble'. (These could include: 'bad' behaviour at the tea table; Mum, Dad and Jessica talking after tea; Jessica hearing her mum and dad having a quarrel; Jessica having her dream; the twins using their notebooks at teatime.) The children then each stick their small pictures onto a bigger one to show the story in the correct sequence.

- Their own 'solution' story: The children could write a story in which a problem is solved.

Co-operative poster

- A healthy, good food chart: First tell the children about the different kinds of food we need for a balanced diet – fat, protein, carbohydrate, fibre – and about how we need to eat a balanced diet. Explain that this is why some foods are healthy foods, containing the protein, fat, fibre, carbohydrates, minerals and vitamins we need, and why some foods are junk foods containing too much fat or sugar.

- Healthy food/junk food: The children stick colourful fruits and vegetables, milk, fish, eggs, oats, etc. in the Healthy food part of the poster and crisps, fizzy drinks, sweets and chocolates in the Junk food part.

The food pictures can be illustrations which the children cut from magazines (using safe scissors) or their own pictures which they draw and colour.

Healthy food

Junk food

5

Signs of Change

Background notes

> ### The child in the story
>
> Amy lives with her mother and grandmother. She attends the local school. She has
> been deaf since she was a small child and she can lip-read and sign very well. She is
> a good friend – kind and loyal. She is an exceptionally intelligent girl.

Additional points

- Many more disabled children could cope in a local school if some
  additional support was provided.

- Children sometimes keep problems at school to themselves. To
  share their problem with an understanding adult can make them
  feel better and be a first step to finding a solution.

Awareness issues implicit in the story

1. The deaf community

Many deaf people do not recognise their deafness as an impairment or defi-
ciency. They claim sign language as equal to any other and a deaf life-style as
complete. In the story, Eddie is unnecessarily sorry for Amy who does not feel
deprived by not hearing, though, once again, we see that the environment

can be disabling, making her (unnecessarily) tired. Clearly, more widespread ability of hearing people to sign (or at least to face a deaf person) would make for a more enabling environment.

2. Isolation

Eddie, however, experiences isolation. His loss of hearing in older age cuts him off from his friends. In company, hearing people often ignore a deaf or hard-of-hearing person, not making any attempt to include him or her in the general conversation. Sadly, the deaf person is treated as too much trouble to include (or even as too stupid to understand)!

3. Carers' concerns

In this, as in several other stories, we see that 'inclusive' solutions can be found. However, we also see that the 'problems' which require solutions are often posed by a disabling environment (e.g. by uniform demands in 'The Magic Shoe Box' or by negative attitudes in 'Across the Pond' and 'A Kind Revenge'). We also see that problems for an impaired child are (often) shared by their care giver (particularly mums). In 'Signs of Change', Amy's mum worries about Amy being tired from the lack of signing offered at her school. Similarly, Dad is concerned for Jack on sports day ('A Kind Revenge'); Ellie's mum shares Ellie's worry about shoes ('The Magic Shoe Box'); Ravi's mum worries about Ravi's 'emotional problems' ('Gifts for Divali'); Connor and Harry's mum worries about their not eating enough ('One and One Make Trouble').

4. Access support

In the story Amy suffered unnecessary fatigue until a signing teaching assistant was appointed to provide support. Ensure that you access available resources for any child who would benefit, for example, support staff, assistive technologies (e.g. listening devices to amplify speech) or learning materials (e.g. big print notes). You should find out, too, about sources of additional funds and allowances.

Further reading

Miles, D. (2004) *British Sign Language: A Beginner's Guide*. London: BBC Books.

Pearson, L. and Lindsay, G. (1987) *Special Needs in the Primary School*. London: NFER/Nelson.

Taylor, S. (2002) *Gifted and Talented Children: A Planning Guide*. London: Jessica Kingsley Publishers.

Storytelling notes

Using the story

As the storyteller, it's likely that you will instinctively structure the timing of the story to provide the children with interesting activities, and will thereby offer them opportunities for stimulation and learning. The plan below is a guide to using the story in an active way, and need not be followed in exactly the sequence that follows – be as creative and flexible with the activities as you like.

Story themes

There are several themes in the story: you could focus on sign language, kindness, isolation, etc.

1. *Introduce the story and theme.* This story is about Amy who is deaf. She is good at lip-reading and sign language. Her mum is good at signing too. When their elderly next-door neighbour, Eddie, loses his hearing, Amy teaches him to use sign language. This story is about what happens as a result.

2. *Vocabulary.* Make sure the children understand the words. Introduce some of these as they colour the picture, and introduce some in the context – as you come to them in the story.

3. *The story.* Show the illustration and tell or read the story.

4. *Talking about the story.* Use some of the questions and discussion points given, and some of your own, to stimulate the children to talk about the story.

5. *Fun activities for active learning.* The activities provide Circle Time games and discussion, things to make, including a co-operative poster for everyone to make together, and 'awareness' activities.

Introduce the story and theme

- Amy, the girl in this story, is deaf.

- She is excellent at lip-reading and signing.

- In a way, sign language is what the story is about.

- If possible show the children a few words in sign language, as well as the story illustration.

Vocabulary

You can introduce some vocabulary as the children colour in the relevant picture. (Pictures can be found in Appendix Two.)

signing – a language using your hands (to speak)

impulsively – without thinking

brave – showing courage

cheerful – showing a happy, joyful mood

lip-read – see what people are saying by reading their mouth movement (without hearing)

glowed – shone

slippered – wearing slippers

tossing – throw up in the air

unbearably – in a way that is difficult to bear

keen – enthusiastic

trance – spell

olden days – long ago time

favour – a good deed to help someone

fascinated – very interested

visiting speaker – someone who comes to give a talk/lecture to a group

tiring – making you tired

a good turn – being kind to someone

The story: Signs of Change

'You look tired, Amy,' signed Mum.

'And, let me tell you, she's eaten less than a mouse,' said Grandma.

Two quick darts of worry darkened Mum's face. She stared at me.

'I'm fine,' I signed, shaking my head. I took a slice of cake just to prove it.

Fortunately Mrs Lester from next door arrived soon after. She chatted to Mum while I did my homework and that kept Mum's attention off me. Working at the kitchen table, I began to drift into sleep. I forced myself awake and looked up just as Mrs Lester was saying, 'He's gone completely deaf now. Can't hear a thing. He doesn't get out, to the pub or anywhere. Just sits in his chair, brooding. He says he feels left to rot like an old mattress on a rubbish tip.'

'I could teach him to sign,' I said impulsively. I like Mr Lester. He's old but good fun – full of jokes and smiles.

'Well, I'm sure you'd cheer him up dear, just by visiting,' said Mrs Lester, taking care to face me. 'He says you're as brave as they come – deaf since you were tiny and always cheerful.'

'It's not brave, Mrs Lester. I can sign and lip-read, see; I don't get left out of anything.'

'Well, pop in on Sunday, dear. That would be very kind.'

*   *   *

On Sunday afternoon I knocked at Mrs Lester's house. She opened the door and led me into her sitting room. Mr Lester was sitting in front of the fire. Bright orange glowed through black coal and he had his slippered feet stretched out to the warmth. He looked up. His face was different, older and thinner than the last time I'd seen him, as though he'd been ill, but he smiled at me, and his nice old face came back again.

'Come and sit by this warm fire, love,' he said, pointing at the armchair on the opposite side of the fireplace. 'Audrey said you might call.'

'Thanks, Mr Lester.'

'You'd better call me Eddie, now. After all, you're the teacher.' He chuckled, which made me smile too.

'OK… Eddie,' I said.

I hadn't noticed that Mrs Lester had left the room but now she came back carrying two plates.

'It's pancake Tuesday next week,' she said, 'but Eddie likes his on the Sunday.'

She gave us both a plate with a pancake on.

'I remember when our lads were small,' Eddie said, 'I was showing off, tossing the pancakes higher and higher until one got stuck on the ceiling. We did laugh.' He chuckled again at the memory, and I joined in.

Mrs Lester touched my arm. 'I knew you'd cheer him up, dear,' she said. 'I'll leave you in peace for an hour.'

She went out again, closing the door. Eddie and I tucked into our pancakes. They were delicious – light and fluffy with lots of lemon and sugar.

Mr Lester carried on telling me stories – mostly about the olden days, when he was a boy. Before I left, I made sure I taught him how to sign 'Goodbye, I'll see you next week.' He looked pleased when I wrote 'Well Done' on his pad. I gave a little wave from the sitting-room door and Eddie waved back. I turned away and then realised I'd left my bag by my chair. I turned back and saw Eddie's face before he knew I was still there. He was staring into the fire and he looked unbearably sad.

Every week after that I went and listened to Eddie's stories, but I always taught him some sign language too. Gradually he got better at signing and began to be really keen to learn it. One Sunday after we had both been staring into the fire in a kind of trance Eddie said, 'What's up, love? Sometimes you look proper worried, is it problems at school?'

'No, not really. I like my school.'

'But… ?'

'Well, the thing is, it's a hearing school. Everyone remembers to face me but, see, Eddie, lip-reading is tiring without any signing.'

'What about a deaf school?'

'It's miles away, for one thing. Anyway, I'd really hate to leave all my friends, now.'

In fact I was worried that Mum might decide my school was too hard for me and make me leave. It made me miserable and scared just to think of it, which is why I tried hard never to show how tired I sometimes felt. The next day, though, there was a parents' evening, and things came to a head.

*　*　*

'Your teacher said you should be doing better, Amy. She asked what time you go to bed in the evening. She's noticed how tired you seem. We think it may be because you have to lip-read all day, love.'

'Don't make me leave, Mum, please.'

Mum sighed. 'Miss Jones said she'd see what she can arrange, dear. We'll have to see what she comes up with.'

That night, even though I was exhausted, I tossed and turned for ages, too worried to sleep. I was afraid they might make me leave my school and all my friends.

The next morning, being tired out, I was glad it was Tuesday. That's when we have a visiting speaker. I find it much easier to lip-read one person. Otherwise I'm turning my head towards one after another, like someone following a football match, and my neck gets stiff and sore.

That Tuesday, after the visitor had gone, our teacher asked for suggestions about who we could invite next. Before I'd had time to think, I shot up my hand. 'Please Miss,' I said, 'our next-door neighbour, Eddie, has wonderful stories about the olden days.'

'That sounds promising,' said Miss Jones. 'Mention it to him, Amy. If he's willing I'll give him a ring.'

'He's deaf, Miss Jones. But you could phone his wife. And Eddie speaks really well, and after the talk I could sign our questions to him.'

'That would be fine,' she said.

That evening I went next door and explained to Eddie and to Mrs Lester.

'The Olden Days,' said Eddie, his eyes twinkling. 'I can certainly talk about that! I'll miss the Club for once. I owe this young lady a favour, that's for sure.'

Mrs Lester nodded her head vigorously in agreement. 'He goes to the day centre now, every afternoon,' she told me. 'They have a deaf group there. They play dominoes and cards, or just have a good natter, and Eddie understands the signing more and more thanks to you.'

'Yeah,' Eddie said, 'and when I get in a muddle we all laugh and my new chums put me right.'

I realised that the old, happy Eddie was really back. It cheered me up, though my own worries soon came crashing back. I knew that Miss Jones was thinking hard about me!

Anyway, the following week, Eddie arrived as our visiting speaker. It seemed strange to see him in my classroom, dressed up in his best suit.

'Mr Lester has very kindly agreed to talk to us about when he was a boy – 80 years ago. About the house he lived in, what they did before television, what they had for their meals and about school in those days. It will be very interesting,' said Miss Jones.

Eddie winked at me and then he began his talk. I was nervous for him, but he was great. He held everyone's attention. Like me, the others were fascinated to listen to how things used to be and to some of Eddie's funny stories about him and his brothers and sisters – all ten of them!

At the end of the talk they asked questions, with me signing them on to Eddie, who still couldn't lip-read very well. At the end Miss Jones thanked him and we all clapped – as we always did, but louder and longer this time. Eddie was smiling and I felt proud of him.

'There's just one more thing I want to say,' he said.

We stopped clapping to listen.

'Amy taught me to sign when I went deaf. Why don't you all learn? It's not too hard and its fun.' He grinned. 'My wife said you'd all love to have a secret language that Mum and Dad can't overhear.'

We all laughed.

'Well, we seem to have run out of visiting speakers,' said Miss Jones. 'We could make it our Tuesday afternoon project if you like?'

'Yeah,' everyone shouted.

After that a sign-language teacher came every Tuesday and taught us; Miss Jones joined in too. It was an easy afternoon for me! Miss Jones also got a signer to come and sit with me for part of the week, to support me. That was what she had been trying to arrange! School became much less tiring. I had more energy and no longer worried that I might get moved to another school. And it was great fun to have the other kids try out signing with me.

'You know what, Mum,' I signed, 'Teaching Eddie helped us both in the end.'

'Yes,' signed Mum, 'You did each other a good turn and everything changed.'

★   ★   ★

One thing stayed the same though. I still visit Eddie on Sundays. It might sound strange, but he's become my very best friend.

Talking about the story

Did the children understand:

- why Amy was always tired after school?

- why Eddie was sad?

- how Eddie's visit to school helped Amy?

Points for discussion

- *Communication.* Everyone needs friends to talk to. This is why sign language is important – and why hearing people could be more understanding by learning to sign or using notes or speaking clearly and directly.

- *Sign language.* Why don't we all learn sign language? Would it be a good idea if we did? If we can't sign, how could we have a conversation with someone who is deaf or hard of hearing? (Face them directly for lip-reading; use a notepad, etc.) How else could we be helpful? (Don't mock; smile a greeting; keep them included in the conversation.)

- *The senses.* Return to the theme of the senses. What senses does a deaf person use? (Sights, tastes, scents, touch.) For hearing people, when is noise a problem? What do you find too noisy? What sounds don't you like?

Resources

The children could look through their books, or through a story, or poem or song anthology to find other relevant stories, poems, rhymes, songs. They could be about beautiful sights, friendship, school, pancakes, language/talking.

STORIES

Leicester, M. (2006) 'The Mystery of the Missing Fish.' In *Stories for Circle Time and Assembly: Developing Literacy Skills and Classroom Values.* London: Routledge/Falmer.

POEMS

Magee, W. (1984) 'The Summer Sun.' In J. Foster (ed.) *A Very First Poetry Book.* Oxford: OUP.

Moore, L. (1980) 'Until I Saw the Sea.' In J. Foster (ed.) *A Second Poetry Book.* Oxford: OUP.

O'Neil, M. (1979) 'What is Red?' In J. Foster (ed.) *A First Poetry Book.* Oxford: OUP.

Fun activities for active learning

Circle Time

- Circle Time game:

(i) Greetings: Teach the children at least two greetings in sign language (e.g. hello; hi there; good day) (see Further reading). Use one of these to greet the child on your left. The children go round the circle giving and receiving a greeting.

(ii) Questions: Teach the children two simple questions and answers:

'What is your name?' / 'My name is X.'

'How are you?' / 'I'm fine. How are you?'

Go round the circle signing these questions and answers.

- Circle Time discussion: Making friends: Eddie felt lonely before he learned to sign because he had no one to 'talk' to. How many of you have been lonely? The children can talk about these experiences. What can we do to make friends? (e.g. smile and say something nice; join in a game; join a club or project or group activity like doing a play or the school choir.) What can we do to be friendly and helpful to a new boy or girl? (Smile; swap names; show them where things are; play with them.) Does anyone feel isolated here? What can we do to help?

Awareness activities

- Communication: Two people: Successful communication requires co-operation from both people. Why? (You have to take turns to speak, not interrupt the other person, not go on for too long before the other person has his or her turn, listen carefully to what the other person says and respond to what he or she says.)

  What is the advantage of writing with another person? (Two sets of ideas and experiences and points of view; spark ideas off each other, etc.)

  In pairs the children could write a dialogue between an older person like Eddie and a younger person like Amy. It could be a grandmother and granddaughter or an elderly uncle visiting his nephew's family at Christmas. Each child could be one of the characters. Together they write down their dialogue, trying to make it an interesting conversation.

- Communication: A group: Do you use a Circle Time object (such as a soft toy or conch shell) for discussions? If not this would be a good opportunity to do so – and thus discourage interruptions in a group discussion.

  Choose a lively topic and remind the children they can only speak when they signal for and *hold* the object.

- What it would be like…?: What are the good things about being deaf? e.g. enjoying beautiful sights even more; learning two languages: English and signing; not being disturbed by noise. What are the bad things? e.g. being left out of a conversation with hearing people; not hearing music.

The children could write a story about someone who is deaf –
showing some of these experiences. Perhaps their deaf hero or
heroine could foil a criminal plot by lip-reading what the criminals
are saying.

Fun things to make or do

- Visiting speakers: Make a list of the clubs and organisations to
  which any of the children belong. (Brownies; Cubs; Church
  groups; choir; sport/leisure clubs – perhaps a family membership;
  dog training night; teams.) The children could talk about what
  they do at that club and what they like about it. As in the story,
  perhaps you could invite leaders and representatives of some of the
  organisations to come and talk to the children about it.

- A 'free' afternoon: You could also ask the children what they like
  doing (reading, painting, football, walks, singing, etc.) Write down
  any of the suggestions that are possible. Let the children vote for
  the first choice (and perhaps for a second choice). You could then
  arrange for that activity to take place.

- Signing picture: The children could each paint a picture of Amy
  teaching Eddie to sign.

- A thank-you card: In the story Amy and Eddie each do the other a
  good turn. Let the children make a thank-you card for someone
  who has done them a good turn, or been kind to them recently, or
  else for someone who cares for them each day. Give each child a
  photocopy of page 83. (Perhaps photocopy onto thin card.) They
  then fold the card along the dotted line. Help them to write the
  person's name and their name on the inside and colour in the
  words. They should then decorate the front by painting (or
  sticking on) a beautiful picture – of flowers for example.

To ....

With Thanks

From ....

Co-operative poster

We sign with our hands and we help with our hands. Give each child a piece of thick white paper, or thin card. Show the children how to draw round their hand. They then colour in this outline. Have paints or crayons with all the correct skin tones of the children – pale pink, light brown, dark brown. When the paint is dry the children cut out their hand. Help each child to write on a 'good deed', e.g. washing up; saying thanks; signing; sharing.

These 'kind hands' can be stuck onto a white sheet – in different directions at random – to make a decorative 'Helping Hands' poster. Alternatively, they can be stuck on in linked pairs to form a long frieze.

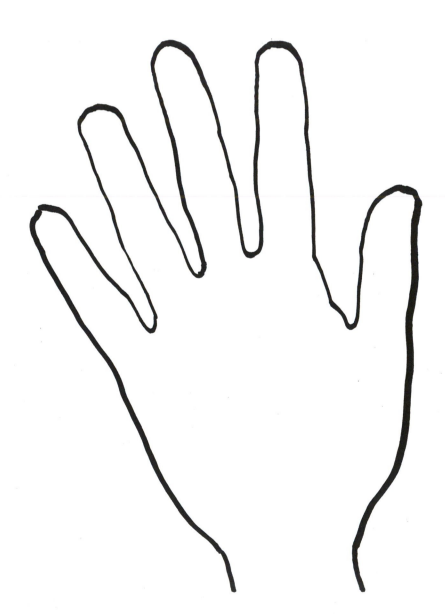

6

Gifts for Divali

Background notes

The child in the story

Ravi loves his pet mice. He likes circles and circular things such as coins and wheels. Ravi is a bright boy with his own way of seeing things – and sometimes his own way of reasoning. He has Asperger's syndrome. People with Asperger's syndrome have some differences in their ways of relating to people and to the world.

Ravi lives with his mum, dad and grandma, and his best friend at school is Anil.

Additional points

- Asian families tend to keep pets less than do white UK families, but Ravi's mum saw how strongly Ravi was attracted by small creatures – especially ones that enjoy running on a wheel.

- This story could be used in religious education projects on religious festivals and celebrations. Interestingly, Ganesha, the Hindu God of abundance and overcoming obstacles, is celebrated at Divali and is portrayed sometimes riding on the back of a little mouse.

- Learning differences are often only differences in degree – on a continuum, as it were, with all children. Certainly the development of empathy, an understanding of other people's feelings and point of view, is a universal developmental need.

Awareness issues implicit in the story

1. Asperger's syndrome

Asperger's syndrome is generally considered to be one of the 'communication disorders'. People with Asperger's syndrome tend to have relatively good verbal language but some non-verbal language problems, and a restricted range of interests. They may have problems with body language and eye contact, and intense fascination with a particular subject or object. Typically a child with Asperger's will have ritualistic behaviours and repetitive body movements. Symptoms include: poor socialization, literal thinking, limited interests, didactive monotone voice, odd behaviours.

2. Problems and strengths

Inevitably, when describing/defining a condition (such as those in the 'Autistic Spectrum') words like 'problem', 'disorder', 'symptoms', 'defects' and 'odd' tend to be used – thus medicalising that particular way of being. This makes it hard for us to recognise that we could instead say that a different way of behaving is not thereby a defective way. As Tony Attwood expresses this:

> The brain is wired differently, not defectively. The child prioritises the pursuit of knowledge, perfection, truth and the understanding of the physical world above feelings and interpersonal experiences. This can lead to valued talents, but also to vulnerabilities in the social world. (Kutscher, Attwood and Wolff 2005; see Further reading.)

3. Explain to the child

It is important that a child diagnosed with Asperger's knows this. He or she will be less likely to become depressed or angry through feeling 'different' and to understand that ridicule or exclusion by other children is not his or her own 'fault'. The child may set about solving his or her social 'problems' by learning how to act in social situations.

4. Different but equal

It is a pity that we so often assume that being different from the majority is to be defective in some way. Rather, within a common framework of respect and kindness, we should celebrate the diversity in our ways of thinking and responding and behaving, and our differences in life-styles and belief.

5. *Equal treatment*

To treat people equally does not always mean treating people the same. It means recognising that we all have the same rights to respect, humane treatment and an enabling education which takes account of our *different* needs, interests and ways of learning.

Further reading

Abberley, P. (2004) 'Disabled people and "normality."'. In J. Swain, French, S., Thomas, C. and Barnes, C. (eds) *Disabling Barriers – Enabling Environments.* Oxford: OUP.

Ariel, C.N. and Naseef, R.A. (2005) *Voices From the Spectrum: Parents, Grandparents, Siblings, People with Autism, and Professionals Share their Wisdom.* London: Jessica Kingsley Publishers.

Kutscher, M.L., Attwood, T. and Wolff, R.R. (2005) *Kids in the Syndrome Mix of ADHD, LD, Asperger's, Tourette's, Bipolar and More! The one stop guide for parents, teachers and other professionals.* London: Jessica Kingsley Publishers.

Storytelling notes

Using the story

As the storyteller, it's likely that you will instinctively structure the timing of the story to provide the children with interesting activities, and will thereby offer them opportunities for stimulation and learning. The plan below is a guide to using the story in an active way, and need not be followed in exactly the sequence that follows – be as creative and flexible with the activities as you like.

Story themes

There are several themes in the story: you could focus on Asperger's syndrome or religious festivals or choosing gifts.

1. *Introduce the story.* In this story we see how Ravi, in spite of his problem of not understanding other people's feelings, manages to work out what gifts to buy his family for Divali. Divali is the Hindu festival of lights. As with the Christian festival of Christmas, part of the Divali celebration includes giving and receiving nice presents.

2. *Vocabulary.* Make sure the children understand the words. Introduce some of these as they colour the picture, and introduce some in context – as you come to them in the story.

3. *The story.* Show the illustration and tell or read the story.

4. *Talking about the story.* Use some of the questions and discussion points given, and some of your own, to stimulate the children to talk about the story.

5. *Fun activities for active learning.* The activities include Circle Time games and discussion, things to make, including a co-operative poster for everyone to make together, and 'awareness' activities.

Introduce the story and theme

- Talk with the children about celebrations, like birthdays – when gifts are given. This provides an opportunity to explain that the various world faiths all have festivals/celebrations. These have their own special rituals but most include the exchange of gifts.

- In the story, Ravi did not intend to give poor gifts when he gave the sugar mice. He didn't yet understand that we all like different things.

Vocabulary

You can introduce some vocabulary as the children colour in the relevant picture. (Pictures can be found in Appendix Two.)

universe – everything there is in space including the earth and all the stars and planets

concentrate – pay great attention

mark – smudge

Divali – Hindu festival of lights

disappear – vanish

cross – angry

heavy – substantial weight

diabetes – condition where your body can't use up sugar very well

emotions – feelings

rocking – gentle movement 'to and fro'

hurried – went quickly

masses – lots

confused – muddled

panic – sudden fright/rush of terror

The story: Gifts for Divali

Of all the things in the universe I like Salt and Pepper the best. They live in a big cage in my small bedroom. One morning last week I woke up while it was still dark and I played with them. For ages I let them run round my fingers from one hand to the other. After that I put them back in their cage and until breakfast time, I watched them run round and round on their wheel.

For breakfast, Mum, Dad and Grandma had muesli. The baby had milk. I had one round of toast with baked beans on top, with as little bean juice as possible. I tried to eat my beans on toast without getting any mark on the plate.

Mum, Dad and Grandma were talking. The baby was making noises. I wasn't listening much because I had to concentrate on not spilling beans on my plate. I did it. The plate was shining clean.

'Are you listening, Ravi?' Mum said.

I raised my head to listen.

'I said here is £10 for buying your Divali gifts'

Mum gave me ten round pound coins. She never gives me paper money now. Once she gave me a £10 note and I tore it up. The paper was not worth ten pounds but ten pounds would disappear if I tore it. Thinking about that gave me a headache. I couldn't stop thinking about it until I tore the paper into tiny pieces. Mum was cross.

I like the heavy pound coins – all looking the same, and all round like a wheel. I like wheels. I made a circle of them round my plate.

'And do your best, Rav. OK?'

'What?'

'You weren't listening again! I said that this year please try your best to buy nice presents.'

Last year I had used the £10 to buy ten pink sugar mice. They were nice. I ate five and that left five for my presents. Mum said that our new baby was too little to eat his and they're too hard for Grandma and Dad doesn't like sweet things and Mum doesn't have much sugar because of her diabetes. Only my friend Anil ate his mouse.

'How will I know what they like or don't like or can eat or can't eat?' I asked.

'You have to think what you would want if you were them.'

'If I were them I wouldn't be me to think it,' I said.

Mum sighed. I thought about what she had said but it gave me a headache. Mum wanted me to buy the right gifts. My teacher had said, 'Buying presents will help his emotional problems.'

My emotional problems are:

- not talking to people much

- not looking at people

- watching my mice too much

- only eating the same things in the same way.

'Are you listening, Ravi?' Mum said.

I raised my head again.

'You can ask me about Grandma's gift and Grandma about the baby. Like that.'

'Anyway, you like working out clues, Ravi,' said Dad. 'Like a detective. Watch us. Pick up clues. Work it out.'

I liked his detective idea.

After breakfast I went to the corner shop and I used five of my coins to buy a notebook and pen, for writing my clues in.

First I sat and watched Grandma and the baby.

'You might as well make yourself useful,' Grandma said. 'Just rock his cradle 'til he falls asleep. He'll be off in the blink of an eye.'

I rocked and rocked. I blinked several times but still he didn't sleep. I didn't mind. I liked rocking the cot. After a long time the baby closed his eyes.

'Well done, Ravi,' Grandma said. She went to sleep too. I looked at them both. It's easier to look at people when they're asleep, but I got no clues to write in my notebook.

I went to the sitting room next, where Dad was reading a book. He reads a lot. I sat and watched him. *Dad likes reading,* I wrote. Every now and then Dad looked at me over the top of his book. The third time he said,

'Haven't you got something to do?'

'I'm being a detective,' I said.

Dad sighed. 'Well, be one somewhere else,' he said. 'Because in any case you don't have to buy one for me.'

I wrote, *Dad doesn't want me to buy him a present.*

I went to the study. Mum was working on her computer. I wrote, *Mum likes her computer.* She stopped and turned to face me.

'Do you want to ask about gift ideas?'

'No,' I said. 'I want to work it out for myself.'

I wanted to solve it like a detective.

I went up to my bedroom. I fed my mice and then I looked at my notebook. My clues were:

- Dad doesn't want me to buy him a present.

- Dad likes reading.

- Mum likes computers.

I wrote some more. *I have £5 left, for five presents. That makes £1 each.*

Writing that made me think of the one-pound shop in the High Street. Everything they sold cost only one pound. I hurried all the way there. I was excited.

I went into the shop and there were masses of things – stacked on shelves and hanging from shelves: toys, books, ornaments, pots, cleaning stuff, smelly stuff, hair slides, nail brushes, make-up, sweets, boxes, cards. Masses and masses of things. There were so many things but the more I looked, the more things I saw and the more confused I felt.

With so many things waiting for me to buy them I just couldn't think. I felt dizzy. I began to panic. I had to get out of the shop.

At bedtime Mum asked again, 'Do you want me to give some suggestions Ravi? It's Divali the day after tomorrow, you know.'

I shook my head. 'No. I want to solve the problem by myself. But I don't mind if you give me another clue for my book.'

Mum thought for a moment. 'Well, don't buy sweets, or anything made of sugar. Except perhaps for Anil.'

That night I had a dream. I was looking in a shop window at a pink sugar mouse. The mouse grew bigger and bigger as I watched. When it was the size of a shoe box it stopped growing, twitched its whiskers and looked at me. I wasn't frightened. I knew it was a friendly mouse because it smiled, and Mum said smiles are friendly.

When I woke up I worked out the answer to my problem. I worked it out like this:

- Don't buy gifts made of sugar.

- Not all mice are made of sugar.

- Some mice are not made of sugar.

- Buy some non-sugar mice.

I was pleased. I could hardly wait to get to the one-pound shop and search for some non-sugar mice.

At the shop, this time the masses of things didn't make me dizzy, because I wasn't looking at everything. I was only looking for non-sugar mice.

The first non-sugar mouse I saw was in the middle of the toy shelf. It was a baby's rattle with a Mickey Mouse head. I liked its big ears and the soft mouse sounds it made when I picked it up. There was a label tied to it showing a baby holding the rattle. I had found the baby's mouse.

To my surprise I saw a notice with the word MOUSE in big red letters. I went to read it. *Novelty Mouse Mats for your computer*, it said. For a computer! Each mat had a picture of a mouse. 'Mum's mouse,' I thought.

I looked and looked but I couldn't see any more mouse gifts. I said to the shop lady, 'I want to buy this mouse rattle and this mouse mat. Do you have any other mouse gifts?'

There was a silence. I wasn't looking at her. I wondered if she was cross. But then she said, 'There's our mouse apron, with a Grandma Mouse.'

I looked at the apron. It had a mouse with little glasses on her nose and a bonnet on her head. A Grandma mouse!

I paid for the rattle, the mouse mat and the apron.

'Oh, and we have these chocolate mice,' the shop lady said.

I liked the chocolate mice. They were like sugar mice only bigger and made of chocolate. I had two pounds left. I bought one for Anil and one for me.

I walked home feeling very, very pleased with myself. I had solved the problem.

'I've got my Divali gifts,' I told Mum. 'One for you, one for the baby, one for Grandma and one for Anil.'

'What about Dad?' she said.

'Dad said he doesn't want one.'

'People say that. He didn't mean it really,' said Mum.

'So he told me a lie?' I said.

'No. It's not really a lie.'

Mice don't say things they don't mean, I thought. I slumped on the table feeling bad. All the good feeling had whooshed out of me. I had no pound coins left. I couldn't solve all my problems now. I had failed.

'Oh well, never mind,' Mum said. 'Time to put away the shopping.'

The shopping was in a bag on the table. It's my job to put things away. I like putting each thing in its correct place. On the big muesli packet it said 'Make Our Bookmark'. Dad likes reading. Bookmarks are for books and books are for reading. I cut out the bookmark for Dad. The only trouble was, it wasn't a mouse gift.

But I'm good at drawing – at copying real things. I got a brown felt-tip pen and I copied my chocolate mouse, six times all down the blank side of the bookmark. It looked good.

The next day we all gave our Divali gifts. Everyone laughed when Mum unwrapped the baby's Mickey Mouse rattle and even more when she opened her own mouse mat. Then they roared with laughter at Grandma's apron and Dad's bookmark.

I didn't understand how my mouse gifts were making a joke. Were they laughing because my gifts were all wrong again?

No. Mum said I had done really well. Each mouse gift was perfect. I felt happy. I had solved the problem.

The Divali gifts I was given were good too. I had a big, round, thin, shiny dark-red toffee lollipop from Anil, warm gloves from Grandma and a detective computer game from Mum and Dad.

Talking about the story

Did the children understand:

- why Ravi gave everyone a sugar mouse?

- why Ravi tore up the £10 note?

- why Ravi made Dad a bookmark?

Points for discussion

- *Difference.* Ravi didn't understand other people's likes and dislikes or jokes very well but he was a kind boy. He wanted to please his mum and he cared well for his pet mice. We are all different with different abilities and disabilities, likes and dislikes. Why is this an advantage? (We can do different things, e.g. different jobs when we are adults; life is more interesting – it would be dull if we were all the same.)

- *Lies and white lies.* Was Dad telling a lie when he said he didn't want a present? What is the difference between a lie (told to deceive) and a white lie (told to be kind) and a social 'lie' (accepted courtesies, e.g. you look nice too; thank you for this nice present)?

Resources

The children could look through their books, or through a story, or poetry or song anthology to find other relevant stories, poems, rhymes, songs. (They could be about mice, wheels, gifts, clues.)

STORIES

Knowles, A. (1988) *The Mice Next Door.* London: Macmillan Children's Books.

Leicester, M. (2003) 'Fireworks for Divali.' In *Stories for Classroom and Assembly: Active Learning in Values Education for Key Stage 1 and 2.* London: Routledge/Falmer.

Plummer, D. (2006) *The Adventures of the Little Tin Tortoise: A Self-Esteem Story with Activities for Teachers, Parents and Carers.* London: Jessica Kingsley Publishers.

POEMS

Ahlberg, A. (1983) 'Picking Teams.' In *Please Mrs Butler.* London: Puffin Books.

Brandreth, G. (1980) 'My Christmas List.' In J. Foster (ed.) *A Second Poetry Book.* Oxford: OUP.

Fun activities for active learning

Circle Time

- Circle Time game: Go round the circle. Each child says what he or she would like for a birthday present. Go round the circle again. Each child names a family member (Dad or Mum or sister, etc.) and says what that person would like. They could also 'make up' a pretend friend and say what that friend would like.

- Circle Time discussion: How do we know what someone else would like? Go round the circle asking for suggestions (e.g. they tell us; we know because they collect… whatever; we know because they were really pleased last time someone sent flowers; we know because they like… sewing/painting/reading, etc.).

  This is also a good opportunity to discuss with the children what they like doing in the time they spend with you. Perhaps they could choose an activity for today.

Awareness activities

- Match the gift: For each child have two sets of cards – one in white and one in red. On each white card write a person or pet and on each red card a matching gift. Mix these up. The children must then match each white card with a red one. Here are some suggestions:

  White cards

Ravi	Father Christmas
Ravi's mum	A pet dog
Ravi's dad	A pet cat
Ravi's mice	Your footballer friend
Your grandmother	A patient in hospital

Red cards

A novelty round notebook	Warm gloves
A painting done by Ravi	A squeaky toy
A book token	Cat treats
A piece of cheese	Grapes
A photo of you	An autograph of David Beckham

- New boy: Ask the children what they could do to help Ravi if he came to their school as a new boy. Discuss their suggestions with them. Ask them which order of importance they would put the following six suggestions:
  - Tell him where things are (less helpful).
  - Show him where things are (helpful).
  - Smile (less helpful).
  - Talk about the film you saw last night (less helpful).
  - Talk about mice (helpful).

  Discuss their answers to explore which actions are helpful and why, which less helpful and why.

Fun things to make or do

- Pet pictures: Looking after our pets: Draw your family pet or if you don't have one, the pet you would like to have.

  How should we treat our pets? (We must feed them correctly and look after them and treat them kindly.) How do we look after dogs? (Stroke them; play with them; take them for walks.) How do we look after mice? (Keep their cage clean; give them mouse food and clean water), etc.
- Gifts to make: Each child can make two bookmarks, one to keep and one to give as a gift. They can also make a picture to take home. For each child photocopy page 98 onto thin white card.

Using safe scissors the children cut out the bookmarks at the top and bottom of the page and decorate the blank sides of these – either using stick-on shapes or by drawing a colourful pattern.

The remaining rectangle can be turned into a picture. They decorate the border and stick a nice picture (or draw one) in the middle. Make two holes where indicated and thread in thin ribbon, or string, for hanging the picture on the wall.

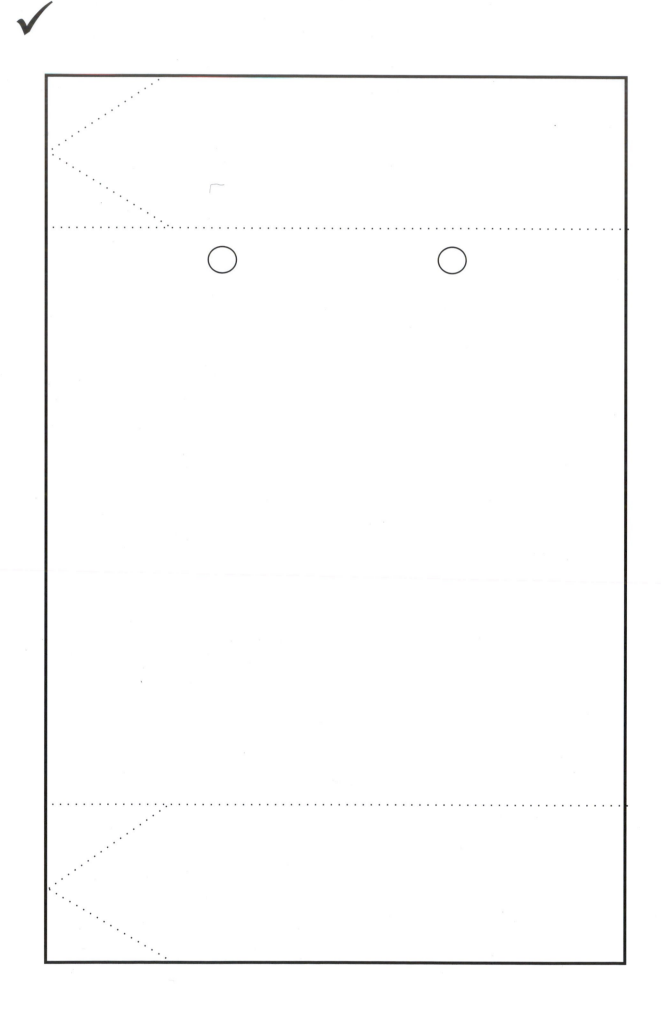

Co-operative poster

Give each child a photocopy of page 100. They turn the oval into a face by adding hair, eyes, nose, mouth, ears. They can add other things if they wish – a hat, earrings, a moustache, glasses.

What does this person like? Help them to add their word – chocolate, football, reading, etc.

On a poster-sized sheet write: 'Different People – Different Likes'.

The children stick their smaller sheets onto the big poster. They will see how many different kinds of people they have drawn.

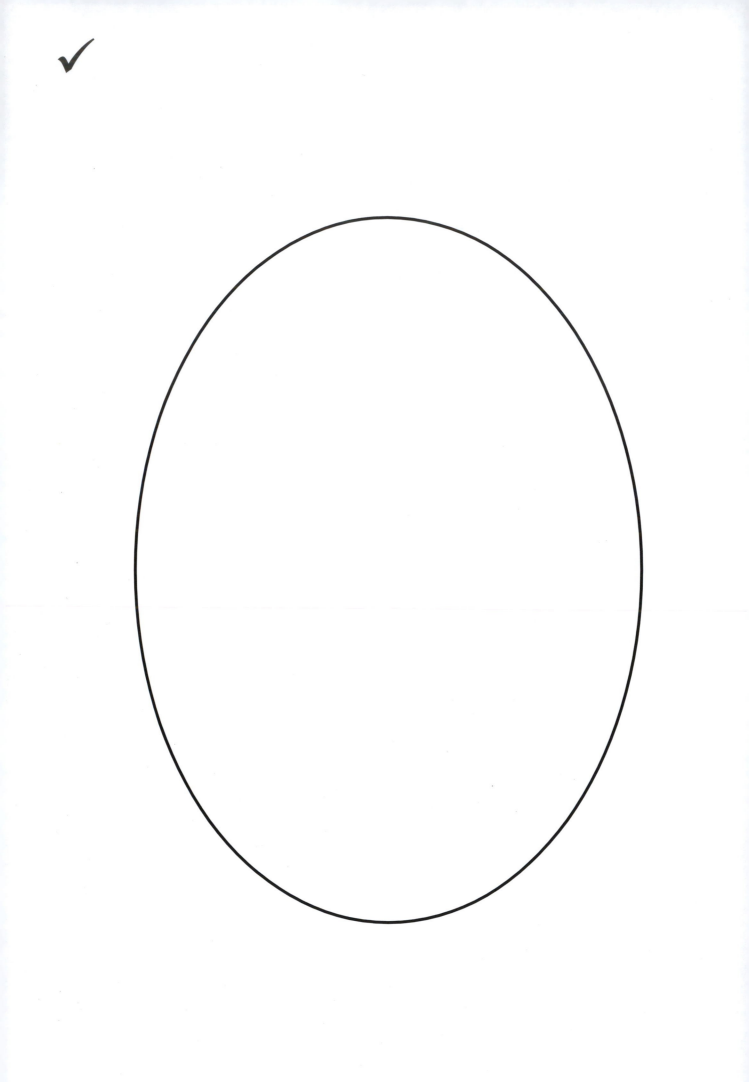

7

Across the Pond

Background notes

The child in the story

Charlotte lives with her Aunty Diana (Dee-Dee, as Charlotte calls her). Her own mother, Dee-Dee's sister, died when Charlotte was a baby. Charlotte is a clever girl. She loves writing and receiving letters. She is very mobile because she is adept at manoeuvring her wheelchair.

Charlotte belongs to a black British family and the story centres on the visit to Britain of her African–American cousin Liza-Marie.

Additional points

- A proportion of disabled children are from minority ethnic groups and in addition to disabled discrimination, will also experience prejudice and discrimination based on ethnicity, including colour and culture-based racism.

- Most children will, at some time, experience feeling 'left out' or 'ignored'. They will understand how Charlotte feels.

Awareness issues implicit in the story

1. 'Her biggest problem is you!'

Several years ago, in a 'Year of the Disabled', an arresting poster depicted a person in a wheelchair with the caption, 'His biggest problem is you'.

A similar thought is encapsulated in 'Does he take sugar?'. In this story Liza-Marie is unsure how to talk to Charlotte, and eventually is surprised to find how clever she is. Disabled people often have the experience of being talked about to a third person – the wheelchair pusher, for example – and mistaken assumptions made about their intelligence. To have an impairment in walking does not, of course, entail intellectual impairment. Across the group, people in wheelchairs will have the same full range of intellectual levels as others.

2. Not a child

Similarly, perhaps because they sit at a lower physical level than a standing person, adult wheelchair users are often treated as children. Indeed some people even adopt the same distinct, slower-paced, bright tone of voice which they use with young children. It must be particularly galling to young adults like Charlotte who are moving into the age group most conscious of not quite being children any longer.

3. Link schemes

There have been many successful link schemes bringing together non-disabled children and disabled children. The non-disabled children enjoy a teaching role with learning disabled children but are also surprised at how many talents the learning disabled children actually have. As we discussed in Chapter 2, learning disabled people have unusual learning profiles – often having difficulty in some areas and strong ability in others. *Physically* disabled children, having the full range of intellectual abilities, can engage in common projects on equal terms and more link schemes of this kind would be a good idea. Further information about these schemes is given in the 'awareness' activities and in *Children's Understanding of Disability* by Ann Lewis (see Further reading).

4. A double loss

Disabled children cope with the loss of a function, and have to do so in a disablist world. In addition, they are, of course, subject to the bereavement, problems, hurts and dilemmas experienced as part of the human condition by everyone. Charlotte, the child in this story, has lost her mother. Fortunately she lives with a loving aunty. It is sad to think of a disabled child coping with impairment without the background support of a loving carer.

5. Pen-pals

Disabled children often experience some social isolation. This may occur because they are bussed away from neighbourhood children to a different school, or, in the case of a wheelchair user, there are still some buildings that are not wheelchair friendly. Sadly many children and adults are prejudiced against the disabled and fail to include them. For these reasons, as we saw in Chapter 1, many disabled children have a particular bond with their pets who provide companionship and acceptance. Perhaps this is also why the giving and receiving of letters and having pen-friends can be much valued too.

Further reading

Lewis, A. (1995) *Children's Understanding of Disability.* London: Routledge.

Matthias, B. and Spiers, D. (1992) *A Handbook on Death and Bereavement: Helping Children Understand.* London: National Library for the Handicapped Child.

Pearpoint, J., Forest, M. and Snow, J. (1992) *The Inclusion Papers: Strategies to Make Inclusion Work.* Toronto: Inclusion Press.

Storytelling notes

Using the story

As the storyteller, it's likely that you will instinctively structure the timing of the story to provide the children with interesting activities, and will thereby offer them opportunities for stimulation and learning. The plan below is a guide to using the story in an active way, and need not be followed in exactly the sequence that follows – be as creative and flexible with the activities as you like.

Story themes

There are several themes in the story. You could focus on wheelchair use, prejudice, garden ponds, America, letter writing, etc.

1. *Introduce the story and theme.* This story is about Charlotte who uses a wheelchair. She wins her cousin Liza-Marie's admiration through a clever idea.

2. *Vocabulary.* Make sure the children understand the words. Introduce some of these as they colour the picture, and introduce some in context – as you come to them in the story.

3. *The story.* Show the illustration and tell or read the story.

4. *Talking about the story.* Use some of the questions and discussion points given, and some of your own, to stimulate the children to talk about the story.

5. *Fun activities for active learning.* The activities include Circle Time games and discussion, things to make, including a co-operative poster for everyone to make together, and 'awareness' activities.

Introduce the story and theme

Liza-Marie is nervous of Charlotte simply because she is in a wheelchair. Probably Liza-Marie has never met a wheelchair user before. She doesn't know that she and Charlotte have a lot in common.

Vocabulary

You can introduce some vocabulary as the children colour in the relevant picture. (Pictures can be found in Appendix Two.)

rattle – clicky noise

pounced – jumped on

relations – people we are related to like parents, cousin, brother, sister

avoiding – ignoring

manoeuvred – moved skilfully

surly – bad tempered

turquoise – a green/blue colour

instinctively – without thinking

slats – criss-crossing wood

glum – sad

twine – thick strong string

intently – with great concentration

mystified – bewildered

smoothed – evened out

darkened – cast a shadow

approach – draw near

The Story: Across the Pond

'It's for you, Char.'

Dee-Dee handed me the envelope and my heart gave a skip of pleasure. I love getting letters. I tore it open.

Dear Charlotte,

Your American cousin, Liza-Marie, is coming to stay for a week in August with her mum, en route to Barcelona. She's the same age as you and I thought you would like to meet each other. I could make up a bed for you in the little downstairs room at the back. Would you like to come and stay? I mentioned it to Di on the phone. She said you would like to get a letter.

Lots of love,

Aunty Shirley

'Dee, Dee,' I shouted, waving the letter, 'I can go, can't I?'

'Is it the letter from Aunty Shirley?' she asked, smiling.

I nodded, an answering smile spreading over my face like spilt cream.

'Of course you can go my love. In fact we'll both go, but you can stay for the whole week.'

'How are they related to us?' I asked.

'Me and Aunty Shirley and Liza-Marie's mum, and your mum, were all sisters,' she said. 'Liza-Marie's mum married an American.'

My own mum had died when I was three. I don't really remember her and my Aunty Di, who I've always called Dee-Dee, is my mum now.

'I'll write to Aunty Shirley and say yes,' I said. 'I can hardly wait! Hey, maybe Liza-Marie will become my first pen-friend.'

Dee-Dee laughed. 'It's going to seem a long time to August,' she said, and she was right. It did.

★   ★   ★

The day came at last however, and I slid into Dee-Dee's car – and we set off.

'Dee-Dee, suppose she doesn't like me?' I said.

'Oh, course she will,' said Dee-Dee, 'and Aunty Shirley told me that Luke plans to take you both to Bobby's big bargain store this afternoon.'

It seemed ages before we arrived but at last we were there. Aunty Shirley hugged us and led us into her big sitting room. Luke was there, and a tall girl in blue jeans.

'Liza-Marie,' said Aunty Shirley, 'this is Charlotte.'

I smiled at my new cousin.

'Hi Liza-Marie.'

She nodded, but without looking at me.

'Is she allowed to go to Bobby's?' she asked.

'Why wouldn't I be?'

It came out sharp and there was a small silence.

'Of course she can go,' said Aunty Shirley.

I wished I hadn't been sharp. I was still hoping like mad that Liza-Marie would be my pen-friend when she went back to New York. Had I blown it?

Aunty Shirley gave us sandwiches and orange juice. Everyone was chatting at once and I tried to join in, but I couldn't help noticing that Liza-Marie avoided talking to me. 'Well, let's go, kids,' said Luke, cutting into my thoughts. Luke is Aunty Shirley's oldest son. He's older than Liza-Marie and me. 'We'll leave Mum and Aunty Di to have a good gossip before Dad gets back with the horror.' The 'horror' was his little brother, Aidan.

* * *

There's a step up to the door at Bobby's. Luke manoeuvred my wheelchair and pushed me in. It's an amazing store. It sells all kinds of cool, cheap things. That day it was very crowded.

'Will she be OK on her own?' Liza-Marie said to Luke.

'Liza-Marie, Charlotte can speak for herself you know,' he said.

Liza-Marie reddened.

'We'll all meet here, near the door, in half an hour,' he suggested.

Liza-Marie moved into the crowd.

'The things I like are upstairs,' said Luke. 'Shall I ask about the lift, Char?'

'No. I'll look round down here,' I said.

I knew from previous visits that the man who runs Bobby's is a bit surly. He never refuses for me to use the lift, but he makes me feel it's a lot of trouble.

'Plus, it's mainly boy's stuff up there, anyhow. You go, Luke.'

'See you soon, then,' he said and he pushed off towards the stairs.

I was quite happy to browse round the aisles near the door. I rummaged in the '50 pence' bargain box. I spotted a big horse-shoe magnet with red ends, the perfect present for Aidan. I bought it and pushed it into my coat pocket, pleased.

Later, when I met up with the others, I could tell that Luke was pleased too.

'Look,' he said, proudly.

He fanned out all the small tools on a key ring he'd bought. There was even a tiny pair of scissors.

'Hey, could you cut this?' Liza-Marie said. She was holding out the price tag on a turquoise writing set.

Luke snipped the cotton.

'There,' he said, with an air of satisfaction.

'That's pretty,' I said, pointing to the turquoise and gold pen in Liza-Marie's set.

'Thanks Luke,' she said.

She still hadn't said a single word to me!

Back at Aunty Shirley's we went into the sunny garden and moved down to the fish pond at the end.

'Why are there wooden slats over the water?' Liza-Marie asked.

'Mum said Aidan might climb the little wall,' Luke said. 'And fall in. But because the water is near the top you can still see the fish. Watch.'

Luke threw a handful of pellets through the bars and we watched the fish rise to gobble up their food.

After that Liza-Marie sat on a corner of the fish pond wall and counted the tools on Luke's new key ring.

'Seven,' she announced. 'Here, Luke.'

She chucked the key ring towards him. Unfortunately it flew past my head and instinctively I raised my arm. The key ring bounced off my hand and dropped, neatly, between the wooden slats. It disappeared into the pond with a 'plop'.

'Oh no,' Luke exclaimed.

Liza-Marie looked horrified.

'It's all your fault,' she said to me. 'I wasn't throwing it to you, was I?'

'Can you take off the slats?' I asked Luke.

He shook his head. 'It's all screwed down. Anyway, the water's deep and Dad won't let me into his precious pond just for a key ring.'

He sounded glum and I looked away, feeling terrible.

My eyes lighted on Aunty Shirley's basket of garden tools. On top was a ball of twine. It gave me an idea.

'Pass the twine, Luke,' I said. 'I've had an idea.'

I tied the twine to the magnet I'd bought. 'Maybe I can fish the key ring out with this,' I said.

'Brilliant idea,' Luke said.

I lowered the magnet into the pond at the spot where the key ring had fallen.

'I can feel something,' I said.

The others watched intently as I lifted up the twine. To my great disappointment, I fished out a big rusty nail. I saw Luke's face change from excited to glum.

'Try again, Char,' he said, without much hope in his voice.

Once more I lowered the magnet. I felt it latch onto something which felt heavier this time.

'I've got something.'

Slowly and carefully I lifted my catch through the wooden slats.

'Yeah,' we all yelled.

The key ring clung dangling from one red end of the magnet. Luke detached it, kissed it with a flourish, grinning, and slipped it into his pocket.

'That was the most fantastic idea, Char,' he said, smiling at me.

At that moment Aunty Shirley called us in for an early dinner and after that Dee-Dee set off for home. Me and Aunty Shirley waved her goodbye. We waved until the car turned the corner. Unexpectedly, watching her go I felt kind of lonely.

I wheeled myself along the path round the side of the house and into the back garden. I wanted to be on my own for a while. Slowly I moved onwards, drawn again to the pond. Something was moving on top of the water in one of the squares made by the slats. I moved closer. Now I could see it was a bottle – with something poking out of the top. I stared in surprise then reached across the pond and pulled out the bottle. It felt cool and water dripped onto my dress. Mystified I saw that someone had screwed a piece of paper into the mouth of the bottle. I smoothed out the paper. It was a letter. To me!

> Dear Charlotte,
>
> That was the most fantastic idea – to fish out Luke's keys with a magnet. Hey, cousin, I'm sorry I blamed you when they plopped in. That wasn't a bit fair. It was me that threw the key ring across the pond. It was my fault really. I hope we can be friends.
>
> Yours, Liza-Marie

A shadow darkened the paper and I looked up and she was there.

'That's OK,' I said, and we smiled.

★   ★   ★

From then on Liza-Marie chatted away to me and called me her cleverest cousin, and in the week she was in England we discovered we both liked exactly the same things – the same books, the same music and the same computer games. Our favourite colour was turquoise, our best school subject was English and our worst one was history. Liza-Marie said she found it boring and, as for me, I could never remember dates. Anyway, we spent a lot of her visit together and I was sorry when she had to leave. Still, three weeks later she wrote to me. After that, whenever a turquoise envelope plopped through the letter box I knew I had another chatty letter from my American pen-pal and friend.

Talking about the story

Did the children understand:

- why Charlotte was keen to become friends with Liza-Marie?

- why Charlotte bought a magnet?

- why Luke couldn't step into the pond to search for his key ring?

- what Charlotte and Liza-Marie had in common?

- why Liza-Marie made her apology in a letter?

Points for discussion

- *Relationships.* Why were Liza-Marie and Charlotte cousins? (Their mothers were sisters.) This is a good opportunity to explore relationship terms with children who are often confused by aunty, uncle, cousin, nephew, niece, step-sister, mother-in-law, etc.

- *Prejudice.* Why didn't Liza-Marie talk to Charlotte at first? This is the opportunity to discuss 'prejudice'. Prejudice is when we make a biased judgement against someone even though we don't know what he or she is really like. These negative thoughts and feelings are often made about disabled people and about black people. Charlotte would not have experienced both kinds of prejudice from her black cousin Liza-Marie; it was disability prejudice she experienced.

- *Structured prejudice (institutional discrimination).* Sometimes it is not only people who show bias. Even buildings can do so! It was not easy for Charlotte to enter Bobby's or to shop upstairs. The way organisations – shops, schools, clubs, etc. – work is also sometimes biased. For example, the libraries may have few books in Braille or big print for people who are visually impaired; schools may exclude disabled children who would cope with a bit of additional support; shops may not cater for special needs; clubs may not find ways of getting in touch with disabled people and may not make them feel welcome and often will not provide necessary access, aides or equipment.

Resources

The children could look through their books, or through a story, or poetry or song anthology to find other relevant stories, poems, rhymes, songs. (They could be about shopping, mobility, fish ponds, letters, etc.)

STORIES

Agard, J. (1979) *Letters for Lettie and Other Stories.* London: Bodely Head.

Andersson, S. (1980) *No Two Zebras are the Same.* London: Lion Publications.

Maris, R. (1989) *In my Garden.* London: Walker Books Ltd.

POEMS

Bradman, T. (1989) 'The Fish.' In *Smile Please.* London: Puffin Books.

Edey, M. (1949) 'August Afternoon.' In J. Foster (ed.) *A First Poetry Book.* Oxford: OUP.

Mass, B. (1977) 'Friendship.' In B. Moses *Poems about You and Me. A Collection of Poems about Values.* London: Hodder Wayland.

Fun activities for active learning

Circle Time

- Circle Time game: Changing Places: You need to notice what things the children have in common. For example you could say, 'everyone wearing a red jumper change places; everyone wearing glasses change places; everyone wearing trainers change places; everyone with a pony-tail'... etc. Now think of things that are different – not for everyone at once! For example, blue and red jumpers change places; short and tall children change places; blue trainers and blue shirt change places... etc. Try to ensure that every child has a change!

- Circle Time discussion: Question/discussion:
  (i) Apologies: Liza-Marie used a letter in a bottle to say she was sorry. How else could she do this? (Encourage suggestions, e.g. say 'I am sorry' to the person; telephone and say 'I am sorry'; smile and say 'can we be friends again?).' What kind of things might we be sorry for? (Encourage suggestions, e.g. being unkind; not sharing; breaking someone else's toy; calling names; hitting; quarrelling, etc.) Go round the circle asking the children to say, 'If I...' (choose an action, e.g. 'broke Sam's pencil') 'I would...' (choose a way of apologising, e.g. say 'I'm sorry, Sam').

  (ii) Prejudice: Build on the previous discussion about prejudice. What groups of people experience prejudice? Have you ever experienced prejudice? Why is prejudice bad? (It is based on ignorance. It hurts people...)

What is the difference between making a mistake and making a prejudiced judgement/decision/idea? (We are willing to correct a mistake but tend to want to stick with a prejudice even against new evidence/information).

Awareness activities

- Boxes: Have three boxes – one huge wrapped in gift paper; one smaller wrapped in silver paper; and one the same as the smaller size wrapped in brown paper. Ask the children which one would you unwrap? (You will get various answers but many will suggest the big box.) Inside the big box have a few other boxes inside each other, with a burst balloon or an empty packet of crisps in the last one. Have an empty sweet wrapper in the silver box and an interesting toy, such as a car, watch, etc. in the brown-paper covered box.

  Discuss with the children how we can make a mistake if we judge people by their appearances and their clothes. Get the children to write (or tell) a story about an ugly person who is kind. What does he or she do? What happens? They could write (or tell) a story about a handsome/pretty person who is mean. What does he or she do and what happens?

- Wheelchair test: Borrow a wheelchair and let the children take turns (one in the wheelchair and one pushing) to go around the building. They should note down any problems or good points (e.g. bad: steps, narrow doors, switches too high, and good: lifts with low buttons, ramps). When all the children have had a turn, the group can share their notes/experiences and talk about these.

- Visiting speaker's test: You could ask an adult wheelchair user to visit the school. He or she could go round the building before speaking to the children. Ask the speaker to talk about what they like, their achievements, and positive and negative attitudes they have experienced from being in a wheelchair. And, also, what obstacles did they find from going around the building?

  Allow time for the children to compare what they found with what the speaker found. Allow time for some general questions.

- A link scheme: Since the Warnock Report (DfES (1978) *Special Educational Needs (Warnock Report)*. London: HMSO) in the UK, there has been much discussion about the integration of disabled children into mainstream schools. What is often overlooked is that there are many ways (and stages) of including disabled children. One way, with many benefits for both sets of children and teachers, is for mainstream schools to link with a special school in a joint project for (say) one afternoon a week. Ann Lewis gives much useful information and advice in *Children's Understanding of Disability* (see Further reading). A period of preparation has been found to be crucial. Overall structured activities have been found to be more successful than free play. However, tasks need to fit both sets of children. In practice you may need to find elements of the overall task suitable for the various children. Activities have included: wax resist painting, potato printing, paper bag puppets, joint writing.

  If any of the children have learning difficulties they can still contribute to such activities, e.g. the mainstream child drips a wax pattern and the learning disabled child paints over this.

  If you are able to arrange a link project this could be interesting and educational for all concerned.

Fun things to make or do

- Alike and different: Tell the children to think of people they know. What do they share? How are they different? Think of you and your best friend. How are you alike? How are you different? All human beings are unique – different from everybody else. But we all have the same needs and rights and feelings. You can make two lists together: 'What we all share' and 'Ways we are different'.

- Make a poem: 'Different but the Same':

  ○ Complete the lines. Give the children a photocopy of page 116 and ask them to complete the third line of each statement, writing something that the two people in each statement have 'the same'.

  ○ Write a poem. Give the children a photocopy of page 117. Read the examples together. Now let the children create their own poems. Each verse will have a 'different' and a 'same' between two people.

You could take the best verse from each child's poem to make one long shared *group poem* to go on the wall.

- Make a beautiful picture: Give each child a sheet of white paper and some green and blue paint. They can mix blue and green to make turquoise. Let each child divide his or her sheet in half (making a faint line in pencil).

  On one side of the paper only, the children make a green, a blue and a turquoise shape. Part of each shape should just touch the line and each other. Before the paint can dry they fold their sheets and gently press their fingers over their paper. Open – and they will find a beautiful, symmetrical, abstract design.

- Letters: The children could write pretend letters:

  ○ Imagine you are writing to the postman. What would you write?

  ○ Imagine you found a letter in a bottle. What would it say?

  ○ Imagine you have a pen-friend in another country. Write him or her a letter, with all your latest news.

And real letters – this is an opportunity for the children to write a real letter – setting it out correctly. Here are two suggestions:

  ○ If another child or adult is ill, each child could write him or her a letter and these could actually be sent.

  ○ If there is something in the local news or local area about which the children have views, with your help they could all write to their MP. Again these letters could be posted.

NB. This is also an opportunity to facilitate a matching up of pen-pals for those children who would like one. You could use a pen-pal organisation or make contact with another group or class similar to, but different from your own (e.g. link an 'ordinary' class and a 'special' school class; or link your group with a similar group).

Co-operative poster

Photocopy page 118 for each child.

The children decorate their fish with colourful patterns. Perhaps you could provide glitter pens, glitter paint and shiny shapes. Once completed, using safe scissors, they cut out their fish.

Finally the children stick their fish onto one large blue sheet to make a colourful 'sea' or 'pond' picture.

✓

Complete these lines

Jack and Jill Went Up the Hill

Jack is a boy

Jill is a girl

They both went _____

Jack Sprat

His wife liked fat meat

Jack liked his lean

Between the two of them

They licked the platter_____

Father Christmas

Rudolph has a shiny nose

The other reindeers don't

They all pull Santa's _____

Two of the Three Little Pigs

One pig made his house of straw

The second out of sticks

Both houses were _____

Shared differences

Make your own 'Different but the Same' poem.
Here are some examples:

Twins

Jack is a boy.

His sister is a girl.

Both are seven years old.

They are twins.

Football

I am white,

My friend is black.

We both like football,

Play for our school team.

Mum and Dad

My dad is tall.

My mum is short.

They live in different houses.

They both love me.

Turquoise pens

Charlotte uses a wheelchair.

Liza-Marie does not.

They both like to write letters

Using turquoise pens.

✓

A fish to decorate

8

The Careless Boy

Background notes

> ### The child in the story
>
> Max is described at school as an 'EBD' child (emotionally and behaviourally disturbed). In this story his behaviour changes as he grows to care more about his music and about a new friend. Max attends a mainstream school and lives with his mum and step-dad.

Additional points

- This story is reprinted by kind permission of Routledge, from *Stories for Circle Time and Assembly: Developing Literacy Skills and Classroom Values* (2006) by Mal Leicester. In that book it is printed alongside a play for children based on the same story.

- In the story we have the hint of a difficult relationship between Max and his step-father. As we indicate below, in practice children who are emotionally and behaviourally distressed have often had traumatic experiences or may currently be coping with difficulties at home.

Awareness issues implicit in the story

1. EBD pupils

EBD pupils are often disruptive, showing little respect for authority. They sometimes get suspended and expelled from school. They are not usually happy children and may have lost their mother or main carer in early childhood. Some children have experienced physical or sexual abuse. Though their behaviour can be frustrating and difficult for the other children and adults in their lives, we have to try to keep in mind that they desperately need help and understanding. Their sufferings have been (possibly still are) part of their problem behaviour, which, without a life-line towards change, will damage their whole life.

2. Emotional distress

Unlike a physical or sensory impairment, there are no obvious physical symptoms of an emotionally distressed child. They have no physical symptoms to elicit our sympathetic desire to support and cherish. Indeed, their very symptoms – behavioural problems such as insolence, disobedience, violence, bullying, rule breaking, etc. – tend to elicit our antagonism, anger and alienation. Unless we recognise these behaviours as stemming from emotional distress, we are unlikely to play a part in helping the child to change.

3. Families

The child in this story has a difficult step-father. It must be said, immediately, that though step relationships can be difficult, there are, of course, many caring and responsible step-mums and dads. As in the real world, the children in these eight stories have a variety of family backgrounds: single mum, single dad, mum and dad, mum and step-dad, mum and grandma, and, in 'Across the Pond', a child fostered (or adopted) by her mother's sister. What matters most for a child is the quality of the care he or she receives. Love is given from within many different family structures. Sadly, however, and for various reasons, not all children are receiving loving care in an on-going, long-term relationship: the loving *attachment* they need for emotional and cognitive flourishing. Teachers and professionals must guard against three common assumptions:

- Not all children have a 'traditional' nuclear family. In fact there are many forms of the family.

- Not all children are properly cared for and loved. Sadly, some experience neglect, indifference, abuse, cruelty.

- Many non-traditional families provide loving care.

Further reading

Barkley, R. (1998) *Your Deficient Child*. New York: Guilford Press.

Bowlby, J. (1990) *A Secure Base: Parent–Child Attachment and Healthy Human Development*. New York, NY: Basic Books.

Rotey, J. and Johnson, C. (1998) *Shadow Syndromes*. New York: Bantam Books.

Storytelling notes

Using the story

As the storyteller, it's likely that you will instinctively structure the timing of the story to provide the children with interesting activities, and will thereby offer them opportunities for stimulation and learning. The plan below is a guide to using the story in an active way, and need not be followed in exactly the sequence that follows – be as creative and flexible with the activities as you like.

Story themes

There are several themes in the story: you could focus on caring for people, friendship, interests, music, etc.

1. *Introduce the story and theme.* The story is about a boy who cares for 'nothing and no-one' becoming a caring boy. It is only if we care about some activities that we will lead interesting lives and only if we care about other people that we learn to be kind.

2. *Vocabulary.* Make sure the children understand the words. Introduce some of these as they colour the picture, and introduce some in the context – as you come to them in the story.

3. *The story.* Show the illustration and tell or read the story.

4. *Talking about the story.* Use some of the questions and discussion points given, and some of your own, to stimulate the children to talk about the story.

5. *Fun activities for active learning.* The activities provide Circle Time and games and discussion, things to make, including a co-operative poster for everyone to make together, and 'awareness' activities.

Introduce the story and theme

If we care for a person – we value them. Children need to learn that all human beings are of value, and deserve to be treated as worthwhile people. We will see how Max, the boy in the story, learns to value his music and his new friend – thus becoming a happier and kinder person himself.

Vocabulary

You can introduce some vocabulary as the children colour the relevant picture. (Pictures can be found in Appendix Two.)

> careless – not looking after things; clumsy
>
> creep – tip-toe, move quietly
>
> slouch – a lazy walk; a drooping walk
>
> gratitude – to be thankful for a favour
>
> brood – keep thinking about something in a moody way
>
> keen – enthusiastic
>
> admiring – appreciative of something of value; thinking well of
>
> coma – unconscious state
>
> progress – improving; getting more skilful at something

Max uses slang words:

> clocked – noticed
>
> nicked – stole
>
> brat – irritating child
>
> sussed – worked out; realised; solved
>
> buzz – great satisfaction; thrill

The story: The Careless Boy

Mum droned on and on; nag, nag, nag. Said I was careless. Said I'd cracked the glass. I shrugged and went to watch the telly. She even came nagging about that.

'Keep it down,' she said. 'He's asleep.'

My step-dad's on nights but day or night we always had to creep round him.

'Here, make yourself useful,' Mum said. 'Take this to Gran's. She's out of milk again.'

Gran loves her tea! Well, I was in no hurry. She'd just have to wait.

I called at Tug's. His mum said he might be up the brook. On the way there I clocked a small kid with a lolly, still wrapped, so I nicked it. The brat yelled loud enough to wake the dead. I scarpered quick and scoffed it at Gran's.

'You took your time,' she said, giving me a sour look.

'There's gratitude, the old tea bag,' I thought. Accidentally on purpose I knocked over her china cup; the one she keeps special for her tea.

'Now see what you've done!' she said, looking upset.

'I don't care,' I said. 'What's the matter with you? It's only a cup!'

'You don't care about anything, Max. That's your trouble,' Gran said.

All the way home I brooded over Gran's words. The old nag-bag was right on this one. I didn't care about anything much, except, funny enough, I did care about not caring, if you see what I mean. It bothered me that I wasn't interested in anything. Not really. Even my stroppy step-dad was keen on football. The truth is, I was bored most of the time. I didn't care much about my family and they didn't care about me. They all look after number one. Sometimes I sussed that the other kids were bothered about things that left me cold. Like if we were all kept in at school because someone wouldn't own up. 'It's not fair,' they muttered to each other. Like it mattered. And they were all mega upset when the class dog died. It was only a dog but even Tug was upset about the dog.

Anyway, I was brooding on all this when I got back home. My step-dad was up by then. He gave me a mean look so I took myself off. I went to the garden shed where I practise my guitar. When I can be bothered that is. Fact is, with practice I could be good.

I hammered out several fast and angry riffs. When I looked up, I found I was staring out of the window, right into the face of the new boy next door. The little kid had climbed up on his side of the fence and was watching me. He grinned, showing a gap in his front teeth, and gave me a thumbs up. I shot out meaning to tell him to clear off, fast.

'That was brill,' he said, before he wobbled and disappeared. I looked over the fence. He'd fallen off a big beach ball that he'd been balancing on and was in a heap on the ground, helpless with laughter. I couldn't help grinning myself. I propped my guitar against the fence and climbed over. The boy watched with admiration.

'You could be in the SAS,' he said, which made me grin some more. I lifted my old guitar over the fence and showed him some fancy chords. I let him try, and even with his small hands, he did OK.

'Tom. Teatime,' someone called from the house.

'Got to go,' he said. 'What's your name?'

'Max,' I said.

'Well thanks, Max, that was cool. Wish I could play like that.'

He raced off and I climbed back over the fence.

After that, Tom and I often met up at the shed. Fact is, I liked having an admiring audience and I was getting better. Sometimes I climbed the fence and gave Tom another go. He loved that. One day his mum was there. She smiled at me.

'I want to thank you, Max,' she said. 'Tom really enjoys your lessons. Look, have this towards some new music.' She handed me a fiver.

'Thanks,' I said, surprised.

We went on our bikes to buy the music. There's a steep hill down to the shops. Showing off, I whizzed along, riding 'no hands' for the last bit. At the music shop I stopped and looked back. Tom, grinning from ear to ear, was copying me. His arms were out like a plane. He wobbled a bit. What happened next was so awful it sometimes replays in my head in slow motion. A car hit Tom's wheel and Tom was flung off his bike, cracking his head against the kerb. I ran to him. I thought he was dead. His eyes were closed and he was very still. A crowd gathered and someone sent for an ambulance. I went with Tom to the hospital. His mum arrived looking white and scared. It turned out that Tom was in a coma.

I was taken home. I didn't tell anyone about the 'no hands', but I couldn't stop thinking about it. If only he hadn't copied me.

About a week later, she knocked at our door.

'Max,' she said. 'Tom's no better. We've tried just about everything to wake him up. The doctor thinks if you played to him on your guitar, it just might bring him round.'

'I'll come right now,' I said. I collected the guitar and she drove me to the hospital. I was jumpy to be there, fretting at every red light.

The kid's face was whiter than the pillow; his freckles dark against his white skin. I felt as though a sharp rock of pain was stuck in my chest.

I played my heart out on that old guitar. I played every day for a week – talking to Tom in between the music. On the eighth day his eyes flickered open. He looked at me and he smiled.

That was the start of Tom getting better. He never got completely right. I mean, it took him longer to make progress on the guitar but we never gave up. We practised in his house once he was home. It was great there. Tom's mum even bought me a red Strat. I love that guitar and with all the practising, I can even play Oasis stuff now. It's a great buzz when I first master a hard chord, or make my Strat sing with grief and joy. And I get that same buzz whenever Tom learns something. He gets it too. He looks up and grins his gap-tooth grin.

Talking about the story

Did the children understand:

- what Max stole?

- why when Max broke the glass Mum said he was careless and Grandma said he didn't care about anything? Did they mean the same thing?

- what things Max valued by the end of the story? (e.g. Tom and Tom's friendship, his guitar, teaching Tom the guitar and their progress.)

- how Max changed as a person (a character change)? Does the hero of a story always change in some way?

Points for discussion

- Was Max responsible for Tom's accident? (Partly. He hadn't meant it to happen but he did show Tom a dangerous thing to do.)

- Max cared about Tom and playing the guitar. What and who do you care about? What is wrong about not caring for anything or anyone?

- What, for you, is the message of this story? (Caring is hard but good; being kind is better than being mean; be careful on the road; good friends care.) The children should understand that there is not just one right answer.

Resources

The children could look through their books, or through a story, or poetry or song anthology to find other relevant stories, poems, rhymes, songs. (They could be about music, accidents, friendship, care.)

STORIES

Boyd, L. (1988) *The Not so Wicked Step-Mother*. London: Viking Children's Books.

Braithwaite, A. (1998) *Being Friends*. Milwaukee, MI: Gareth Stevens Publishing.

Wilde, O. (1982) *The Selfish Giant*. London: Puffin Books.

POEMS

Ahlberg, A. (1983) 'I Did a Bad Thing Once.' In *Please Mrs Butler*. London: Puffin Books.

Kitching, J. (1980) 'Gran.' In J. Foster (ed.) *A Second Poetry Book*. Oxford: OUP.

Fun activities for active learning

Circle Time

- Circle Time game: Ask the children to think of something they like that begins with the same letter as their name. Go round the circle for these likes, e.g. Max could say 'I like music.' Keep going around until the children run out of words.

- Circle Time discussion: Mean and kind: Max was mean when he broke Gran's special cup. Max was kind when he played his guitar all day long to help Tom.

  Ask the children to give some other examples of mean acts. Why are they mean?

  Ask the children to give some examples of kind acts. Why are they kind?

  Give positive comments on kind acts which involve assisting someone vulnerable (e.g. a new boy, a sick person, a disabled person, a person being bullied). For example, say 'Yes. That's a good idea.' Finally go round the circle asking the children to say something mean that begins with the same letter as their name, for example Max could say 'It is mean to make someone miserable.' Then go round asking them to say something kind that begins with the same letter as their name. Max could say 'It is kind to make a Get Well card for someone.' (Allow a little thinking time before going round the circle for these sentences.)

Awareness activities

- How to help: 'The Careless Boy' is story number eight. The previous stories have featured:

  ○ Tom, who is blind ('Tom's Famous Bridge'). He is good at drumming and loves his dog, Scamp.

- Ellie, who has learning difficulties and a co-ordination problem ('The Magic Shoe Box'). Ellie is a good friend. She is rather shy but was prepared to stand up for herself at the end.

- Jack, who uses sticks to walk ('A Kind Revenge'). Jack is also a good friend. He is good at making people laugh.

- Harry and Connor, who have ADHD ('One and One Make Trouble'). They are both very good at maths.

- Amy, who is deaf ('Signs of Change'). She is very intelligent and a good teacher and excellent at signing and lip-reading.

- Ravi, who has Asperger's syndrome ('Gifts for Divali'). He loves his mice and is fascinated by circles and wheels.

- Charlotte, who uses a wheelchair ('Across the Pond'). She loves writing letters.

These eight characters can be used in an awareness activity about how to be kind and useful to a variety of people. Ask the children to use their imagination to think of ways they could be kind or useful to:

- **Tom:** Give him a tape with drum music; praise his dog; offer to accompany him on a dog walk, allowing him to take your arm when Scamp is off the lead.

- **Ellie:** Quietly offer to help Ellie with a task that requires co-ordination skills, e.g. tying a knot if she was making the picture in Chapter 6; praising Ellie for the things she is good at; giving her a nice smile and asking what she did at the weekend.

- **Jack:** Laughing at his jokes; sticking up for him against a bully; passing him his sticks if one falls down; calling him by his proper name, Jack.

- **Harry and Connor:** Being understanding if they are fidgety; telling them a joke or a story with numbers in it; trying not to quarrel with them about something they do because of being impulsive.

- **Amy:** Facing Amy when talking; learning some sign language to talk to Amy; pointing out a beautiful flower or a rainbow in the sky.

- **Ravi:** Showing him a picture of interesting vehicles with big and tiny wheels; telling him something about a mouse; wishing him Happy Divali.

- ○ **Charlotte:** Helping her to manoeuvre her wheelchair up a step; writing her a letter; showing her a nice picture with lots of turquoise in it.

- Help me to stop: Have a general discussion of why bullying is bad. Discuss why people might bully. Ask for suggestions about how we could help ourselves not to be a bully (e.g. don't be in a bullying gang; make friends with someone kind; try to find a kind thing to do or say to someone when you are tempted to bully; ask your teacher to help you).

  Are there bad behaviours we find it difficult not to do? (If someone makes a suggestion, such as shouting, say, 'Yes, it can be hard never to shout.') Don't be surprised if no one volunteers a suggestion, and have some ideas yourself (e.g. interrupting, quarrelling…). For each suggestion discuss: how can we help ourselves to stop that behaviour? How can we help someone else?

Things to make or do

- A class 'kind deed' list: You could start a class 'kind deed' list – either in a notebook or on the wall. Encourage the children to record their kind deeds and the kind deeds of other children (e.g. today I helped to pick up litter in the playground; today I helped Katy from nursery class to do up her coat buttons; today Aiden helped Tom clear up his paints; today Amy shared her sweets with me).

- Write a story: The children could write a story about a kind person or about a mean person or a story with both. Explain that we usually like the kind character and don't like the mean one.

- Teacher: Amy taught sign language to Eddie. Max taught Tom how to play the guitar. We often get better at something by teaching it to someone else. Find out things the children know about or skills which they have and let them take turns to be a teacher.

Co-operative poster

- Things we value: You will need to have collected some catalogues, newspapers, magazines, cards, etc.

The children can look through these to find something they value. The picture might represent a value, e.g. a lollipop lady represents kindness and safety (explain this). Remind the children that when we value something we like it but we also think it is a worthwhile thing that we all value (e.g. not everyone likes chocolate even though I like it, but we all value food; not everyone likes football but we all value exercise, fresh air and sunshine).

The children cut out the picture they have found. These are then pasted onto a class poster of 'Things we value'.

- Nature collage: Max looked for his friend 'at the brook'. (What is a 'brook'?) Many children value outings/playing out in the fields. Talk about the value of the natural world and what we see there. Arrange to take the children on a nature walk. (It need not be far, e.g. round the school grounds.) The children collect natural objects – twigs, various shapes of leaf, small stones. Let the children stick their objects onto a large sheet of sticky paper to form a 'nature collage'.

My Experiences

Jane Dover

Introduction *by Mal Leicester*

'My Experiences' was written by my daughter who wanted to share her experiences growing up as a disabled person and to make suggestions helpful to other disabled people. It seemed right that a book of disability-aware stories should include this authentic voice of a disabled person, telling her real-life story from childhood through to adulthood. Moreover, the inclusion of Jane's experiences as an adult reminds us that disabling prejudice and discrimination disadvantage disabled people beyond childhood. (Deepening our awareness and understanding of their lifelong oppression should, surely, be part of professional and personal lifelong learning.)

Reading Jane's words I saw where some of my story ideas had come from, for example the love of Scamp in 'Tom's Famous Bridge'; the problem with shoes in 'The Magic Shoe Box'; and the pain of name-calling and the importance of friendship in 'A Kind Revenge'. Fiction and non-fiction are as interrelated as sunlight and air and never fully separable. Jane's brief memoir tells the truth about how *she* experienced a variety of events that actually happened, while my stories seek to tell, through particular 'made up' characters and events, some general truths about the kind of experiences that disabled children (indeed any child) may have.

Jane's account is in her own words. (She has always been highly articulate.) It is followed by brief comments from me, to provide a parental perspective. My personal self and my professional self are as interrelated and inseparable as the fiction and non-fiction mentioned above. Thus, though I write as a professional educator, at a deeper level, at my very core, I am the mother of a disabled daughter. Together we lived through the hell of Jane's brain tumour, and we have both experienced prejudice, discrimination, hostility and exclusion attendant upon the impairments stemming from that cancer and its terrible but lifesaving treatment. My career-long commitment to a more just and humane society is partly fuelled, and strengthened, by my anger on Jane's behalf, by my admiration for her courage and resilience and by my love.

My experiences *by Jane Dover*

Introduction

The reason I decided to write this is because of my experiences as a disabled person: first at school and being bullied because of the difficulties my brain tumour left me with. Having to deal with people's attitudes towards me. Because of the treatment I had to have to cure me, which killed off the hair follicles at the back of my head, which stopped my hair from growing back and being stared at because of it, and horrid comments being made.

Some of the comments I used to get said were, 'Oh look at her she's got no hair,' and 'Why is she so small?' which made me feel really hurt, but I could not say anything because then I would get, 'why is she so small and fat,' because of my growth problems. I felt I could not tell mum about it and blamed myself for it.

When I was younger I used to get mistaken by people for a young 12-year-old girl, which helped in some situations, but not all.

Through these experiences, which I write about in this book, I hope to make other people, who might go on to bully other children, realise just how hurtful their comments can be once they have said them, and what it might be like if it happened to them and their family. Or if they were on the receiving end of the bullying.

Section one: school years

My mum told me that the health centre did not realise why I kept falling over after I had learned to walk. I was 18 months old. I saw my own doctor who diagnosed my tumour.

After my illness and the operation to remove the tumour, with the help of my horse on wheels I learned to walk again, but because my balance was affected by the tumour, which meant that I could not ride a bike without sta- bilisers and even then I fell off, was made fun of by the other children because I did not have what they classed as a normal bike like theirs.

My illness also made it hard to lose weight and I was made fun of and still am, and this hurt a lot when they made fun of me.

I never really got on with W and his two sisters who constantly made fun of me which hurt a lot. My two very close friends were Hazel from across the road and Emma. I enjoyed going to a birthday at Emma's house and having my friends around to play at my house and in my little house which mum had built at the back of our house.

I remember trying to ride a big rocking horse in Christie Hospital where I went for my check-ups after my operation for my cancer and having problems because of my balance. But I kept trying and did in the end ride the horse, which just proves that you can do something if you have the determination to do, so I did.

I remember cleaning my mum's little red mini with the help of my friends and my grandad. We washed and waxed it 'til it shone.

When we lived at Nicolas Road in Manchester, my first school was a mainstream school and I found it very hard to make friends because I was bullied by a horrid girl in my class who used to take me over to a corner and throw me on to a mat and while I was on the mat she used to sit on my chest and I found it hard to breath. She used to do this on regular occasions and I did not like this.

My second school was better because it was a school for disabled students. I made lots of friends and liked the teachers.

I remember a good experience at school was when our class had an Easter egg hunt and we all had to search around the grounds of the school for clues. Our PE teacher gave us a good clue and one of my friends knew where to look to find it. But, I had a bad experience where I was given some very hard sums to do by my teacher, who I did not like, and because I had trouble doing them, my friends helped me to do them and the teacher found out and pulled me out of the headmistress's room and I was really embarrassed about it because she told the whole class and they made fun of me.

My illness had left me with a co-ordination problem. I found PE really hard and I could not climb on the wooden horse and so I felt really upset when I saw the other children climbing it because I found it too high. I also remember knocking over a display and I got told off for it which upset me because it was not my fault.

I remember the physio making me walk with my feet straight and because I was having problems and my foot would not do what I wanted, she made me do it again and again because I kept getting it wrong, which was not my fault. I also remember the physiotherapist making me do exercises which I did not need to do and if I got them wrong or did not do enough she made me do them again until I did, with my friend Helen Smith who went on to go to the same college as me in Cheltenham.

I remember that the school put me on a diet and all they let me have for pudding was crackers and cheese and I was not allowed to eat anything else for my puddings because they said my mum had told them to put me on a diet, which was not true, and so I felt really left out when all the other children had chocolate sponge and custard, which was my favourite. And one lunchtime when no other students were at my table, I thought one piece won't hurt me, so I had one small slice and somehow they found out and I was put back on crackers and cheese.

I was sad to leave all my friends but was given a lovely book which was signed by the headmistress, Miss Williams.

I started a new school in Birmingham; again, this was a special school for students who were physically disabled. I did not like the area, it was very rough. I was picked up by minibus and brought home again at home time.

I liked the school in Birmingham and made lots of new friends quickly. Everyone was very friendly and I got on well with them. I liked my teachers and the lessons but not the area we lived in which was a flat but in a very rough area. I had no friends to play with and nowhere nice and safe to play.

I remember going to where my mum worked one day after school and having to wait until she had finished work before we could go home. I remember a friend of my mum's who worked there called Azra. She was an Asian lady who was very nice and a nice person to talk to. I remember giving her my pet budgie after my other had died because I did not want him to be on his own. She was very pleased.

We moved to Bristol and I started a new school, again a special school. I made friends easily with Lee and his sister Lynn, Brian and his sister Marie and Sharon and her brother Terry.

I used to go down to the local city farm, which my uncle and a few friends helped to build it from nothing, that was across the road from our house and sometimes helped feed the animals which I really enjoyed. They had donkeys, pigs, goats, rabbits and sheep. I remember my Uncle Eddie bringing a young lamb home with him one night because its mother had rejected it. We had to take turns in feeding it with a bottle until it was old enough to fend for itself back at the farm and it slept in our bath.

My uncle brought home with him one night, a dead pig, for the freezer, which he made a joke of and said that is what we were having for tea. That put me off meat for good and I became a vegetarian and have never eaten meat since.

I liked my teachers and my headmaster. I liked doing cookery classes. I made friends with Sean and we became very close.

Section two: college years

I left school at 16 and went to the National Star Centre College for Disabled Youth. I took an exam in spoken English and got two credits and one pass. I also took my life-saving skills in swimming stage one and passed.

I liked doing home economics and used to make my own Christmas cake and Christmas pudding at Christmas time, which helped my mum because she did not need to make one or buy one.

Sometimes students went home for the weekend. Students furthered their independence by being at the college and even learned to do their own washing on the college campus. I also liked doing horticulture and I learned a lot, including how to plant up hanging baskets.

I started to do my Duke of Edinburgh Award, which I enjoyed doing but never got the chance to finish it, even after leaving college.

I remember doing English lessons. The College has taught me to become more independent. When students first started at the College, you spent your first term on the College campus and then you were chosen to go to one of the houses off campus to further your independence.

The College had the laundry room where the more independent students could take their washing to be done if they were not in accommodation where there was a washing machine and dryer. In my first term I shared a room in the Moose Bungalow.

I remember one summer that we were there, we had a drought and all our water dried up, even our drinks machine, so we had to get the Gloucestershire Fire Brigade to come to the College to fill all our wheelie bins up with water so that all the students could have a drink, which was important because some of the students had to drink more than others because of their disability and medical history and were told to by their doctor and apart from meal times and break times after dinner or lessons, which was the only time students could get a drink, the only other place on the College campus was the building we called the concourse which had a drinks machine where you could get coffee, tea, soup and blackcurrant.

I remember an incident at college where students in my class were told about a holiday that some students would be chosen to go on but only a few selected to go. While we were there we had to take in turns to lay the table for meal times. This one time I remember that no one offered to help lay the table for the next meal and so I offered to do it. Then I started having problems remembering how many people were there to lay the table for meal times and got very upset about it because of my number concept which they did not understand and this made things worse because they would not leave me alone until I had laid the table. At one point I was so upset that I went into our bedroom to get away from everyone who was looking at me because I had volunteered to lay the table but one of the members of staff brought me back into the dining room and I felt really small because of it.

Section three: training years

After leaving the National Star Centre College I went on a youth training scheme with Warwickshire Training.

While I was on the YTS Scheme, I was asked one day to carry a very heavy parcel which we were going to take to the centre, ready for the new trainees when they started the course. I didn't get very far because I dropped the parcel and when I went to pick it up, I twisted my left ankle and could not put any weight on it.

After C, who worked at the centre, took me to hospital and they strapped my ankle and put a supportive bandage on it, he took me home where I had to rest it. Getting up and down stairs at home was hard and sometimes when I forgot that I had hurt my ankle and put my full weight on it, it really hurt and stopped me from doing it. I had to get sick notes off my doctor while I was at home to send in to the centre. The YTS scheme apologised for giving me a parcel that was too heavy.

My ankle has never been the same since I tore my ligament. This has made my left ankle very weak and I keep going over on it, which weakens it even more.

My first placement was at Waverley Road Day Centre where I helped make refreshments when people first arrived and serve dinner at dinnertime and went to the local shops for people who wanted anything.

I also helped another group who came to the centre on a different day of the week, served meals and played dominoes and bingo with them after dinner. Sometimes I went on the bus to pick people up from their house to bring them to the day centre. When I left there, I went on to work at the Oxfam Charity Shop at the top of the Parade in Leamington where I helped sort clothes and get them ready for putting on a hanger ready to put out in the shops. Sometimes I worked on the till. I also learned to deal with the general public which sometimes was very hard.

I then left there and went on to work at Trading Standards where I helped answer the telephone and dealt with incoming post and sometimes put phone calls through to people in the offices above Trading Standards.

I remember a bad situation that happened at Trading Standards where the person I worked with and my tutor started talking about what I was wearing and my shoes were not suitable for what I was wearing and did not go with my clothes. When my mum found out, she was very angry with them for doing that.

One day when I came into my work placement, my tutor and another worker at Trading Standards were discussing my clothes and my shoes, which they said were not suitable for me to wear together. This upset me a great deal as I always had difficulty finding clothes that would fit me because of always being slightly plump and not in my size and shoes that were comfortable to wear because one of my feet being bigger than the other, and my illness made it harder to tie shoelaces on other shoes. They asked me if I had any other shoes I could wear instead, which I had not, and they would not stop talking about it. They said that they would talk to my mum about it which upset me because I would never talk to them about what they were wearing in front of them, which I feel they could have done when I was not there.

I remember another bad experience that I had at the centre was after a new trainee started on our course. She asked some of us for money and her excuse when asked why she wanted the money, she said that her Aunty was ill and she needed to go and see her, then she said she needed more money because we had not given her enough, when really she had spent it on some boots that she had seen that she wanted.

I remember another bad experience that happened on my way to work one day. I was waiting for my bus to take me to the Youth Centre and I left the house early enough to walk up the parade in Leamington to catch the bus to Warwick to the Youth Centre and had been waiting for a while when every other bus came except the right one to take me to Warwick. When it finally arrived, it meant that I got to the centre late and when I tried to explain to my tutor why I was late, she did not believe me, even though I was telling the truth. Neither did my personal tutor or the head of the centre. So when I got home, I told my mum and she was very cross with them for not listening to me about my bus being late and making me late getting to the Youth Centre.

When new students start college, it's frightening and overwhelming enough, but for students with a disability it can be even more daunting and it does not help them if teachers don't tell you where the classrooms are or the toilets. This happened to me and so I want to try and say to any disabled person who is thinking of starting college or university to ask a member of staff, including teachers, questions and to get as much information about where things are at the college or university so that bad experiences like that don't happen to them.

I remember another bad occasion where I had agreed to raise money for a charity 'Dreams come True' and my mum wanted me to put the money in the bank because she did not want a lot of money in the house, so during my lunch break I went to the bank, but it took longer to bank the money and when I went back to work I got told off by my manager for taking too long a lunch break because I was meant to be back by 1.30 and got back later than that. I was really upset when I got home and when I told mum she was very angry with her for being cross with me for being late back from lunch because I had to bank the money which took up all my time and so I had to go without any dinner and stayed hungry until teatime. She came in with me the next day and had a word with her about my disability with time and numbers but I don't think it made much of a difference.

When I left Warwickshire Training, I went to see someone who ran the centre and was told by her that her training centre was different to Warwickshire Training but this turned out not to be true. After my interview I was asked what my interests were, and what would I like to do if I decided to start a placement there. I said that I liked animals and children, and would like to either work with children in a school or playgroup, or animals in a vet's surgery or animal sanctuary, but I ended up packing Christmas stockings for cats.

Not being given a choice was bad enough, but being disabled and having had one bad experience on one YTS scheme was even worse because I felt it was happening all over again. I felt that the staff handled the situation very badly, because I was told that the scheme was different to the YTS scheme and they seemed very understanding when I was interviewed, but did not explain that I would be treated differently to other students, without a disability, which is discrimination against disabled people. Why should we be treated any differently to able-bodied people?

As part of the training on the scheme, the students had to go on an activity course. One was repairing a dry stone wall, abseiling down the face of a cliff and canoeing. We also had to build a raft out of old oil drums and string, which when it was complete we had to sail on the river.

Disabled people who go on YTS schemes should not be made to do activities if they have a bad back or other disability that means they will suffer a lot of pain.

After I left the YTS scheme I got a placement with the Guide Dogs for the Blind in Leamington on a voluntary basis through the Shaw Trust where I worked in the kennels with the dogs. I helped groom the dogs, feed the dogs and walk the dogs. I also helped clean the kennels and prepared the meals for the next day. Some of the dogs needed a lot of supervision when we fed them because they did not digest their food properly. I really enjoyed working there and getting to know the dogs.

I also began voluntary work in the Shaw Trust Charity Shop because it was my way of saying thank you to Jill for getting the placement for me.

Section four: independence

For two years I lived with an old college friend in Norfolk to further my independence away from home. She then decided that she wanted to try living on her own so I moved back to Leamington in my own flat at the top of my mum's house.

I bought my first Shetland Sheep Dog 'Inky'. I have had lots of pleasure from her. Walking both Inky and Shandy helped to straighten my back as they pulled gently on the double lead I had bought them. They became part of my family.

When I joined my local PHAB (Physically Handicapped and Able-Bodied) Club I felt very at ease and made lots of new friends who had disabilities, and some were able-bodied and unlike both the training schemes, I was not made to feel I had to do anything that I did not want to do and was treated like an adult for the first time in a long while. Other people in society need to realise that even though a person may have a disability, we can do some things that they can and deserve to be treated with respect. There should be more clubs like PHAB clubs in different counties and not just Warwick; they treat disabled people like adults and not children, which is very degrading and can make us feel very humiliated by the general public.

We raised all our own funds by holding darts marathons at the local pub and our local flag day in Leamington. I ran a tuck shop selling refreshments such as tea, coffee, hot chocolate, crisps and chocolate and orange juice. I held a sponsored dog walk and coffee morning to raise money for the club and Kieron Groves did a sponsored bike ride. We were both given a certificate by the club to say thank you for raising the money for the club.

I met Steve at PHAB. Steve and I became very close. We got engaged on February 14th 1995 and got married in July 1995. We had our reception at the Riverside Restaurant in the Jephson Gardens and our honeymoon in Jersey. While we were there we visited the German underground hospital and the Sealife Centre. We lived in the flat on the top of my mum's house for a year until we bought our first house where we lived for five years. We moved to Nottingham and decided to start a family and had treatment at the Park Hospital. We like our house and garden in Nottingham and enjoy keeping our garden tidy and looking after our house and my little Shetland sheep dog and fish.

Inky likes our garden as we only had a yard at our house in Leamington. We were sorry to leave PHAB and miss our friends, but felt it was the right thing to do because of Steve's illness was made worse by his last employers who threw water over him and locked him in the toilets.

Steve was very badly bullied at the nursing home where he used to work which made him feel even worse in himself which did not help his confidence. This meant that he dreaded going into work every day because of these bullies, and he used to tell me when he came home from work every night dreading the next morning because he knew what would happen the next day at work. I also had to build up his confidence.

I have learned from my experiences and it does not matter what mean people think or say. I have not had any horrid things said to me since the move to Nottingham.

We were then expecting our first baby.

Because of my disability, I have found that my back pain got worse with the weight of the baby and my headaches have got worse because there is more blood being pumped around my body because of the baby. Other disabled women may find that they may have the same problems as me, especially if they aren't very tall as height can help in pregnancy to carry the baby's weight.

Section five: the future

Our baby son is now two years old. He is called Aidan. He is a very happy baby and is very laid back about everything. I had Aidan in the Nottingham Hospital and was in hospital for five days.

Because I have co-ordination difficulties I had problems lifting Aidan out of his cot when he cried or wanted feeding and changing his nappy, and did not feel very confident about it. I found that the staff did not understand this so I did not get as much help as I should have done because they expected me to be able to feed Aidan and to lift him out of his cot and change his nappy, which I could not do because of my disability. So it was better when I got home because I felt more relaxed as I had help from my mum at first until I felt more confident with Aidan in my own home with some help from my husband Steve.

When Aidan was born he was six pounds nine ounces, but lost some of his birth weight after he came home. Since then he has doubled his birth weight.

Aidan is such a happy baby and gives us some lovely smiles, especially in the morning before his breakfast. He gives us so much pleasure out of life and he loves his walks and to be played with and talked with. Having had Aidan proves that disabled people can have children and it's not impossible like some people think. Steve is a wonderful father to Aidan and we love Aidan very much.

Section six: recommendations

1. FRIENDS AND FAMILY

- Parents should make their children feel at ease when approaching the subject of bullying because some children feel awkward and embarrassed about talking about being bullied at school.

- If parents think that their children are being bullied at school, they should encourage them to talk about it in case they think they will be told off.

- I have always loved creatures who do not make judgmental remarks. I have had a lot of joy from my dog, Inky. I would recommend parents to let their disabled child have a pet.

- Disabled children should be involved in everything and help, like I used to make the Christmas cake for Mum. They should be given as much independence as possible.

2. GENERAL PUBLIC

- Parents should teach their children that it is not nice to say rude and hurtful things about people who have a disability or disfigurement or who are different to other people.

- They should also teach them not to stare.

3. TEACHERS

- Teachers should be able to find a way to talk sensitively about bullying with the parents and the headmaster or headmistress and the children to come to some sort of solution to the bullying and real reason the bullying started in the first place.

- Talk to the parents of the other children if there are problems between the children and any bad comments are being made.

- If a child finds something hard to do, like my lack of number concepts, the teacher should never humiliate the child in front of the other children. She should be sympathetic and build up confidence.

4. TRAINING

- As part of being on the YTS scheme, I had to go to the local college in Leamington for several days a week, when I wasn't at my placement at the centre. I did not like the college because I did not know my way around or where the classrooms were and no-one told me where the toilets were, so I ended up looking for both the classroom and the ladies toilets, which I could not find, and ended up having an accident and had to go home early to change my clothes, I was really embarrassed about it. This also taught me that the college did not know how to include disabled people and that they did not have the right equipment, apart from a lift, to help disabled people who needed extra help. It was alright for the able-bodied students because they had what they needed there but not disabled students.

- I found the activity course very hard to do because of my disability and my back was very painful after sitting in the canoe for such a long time.

- I went for an interview at the centre before I started there and was asked what I wanted to do as a placement and I said that I liked working with children in school classroom or animals in a vet's practice because that is what I am good at but was not given the choice and was told that the only placements available to me were cleaning toilets in a school and packing Christmas stockings for cats and packing them in boxes ready to be put in the shops. I don't feel that they listened to me at the interview. This really upset me because I was told that this training scheme was different from the first one. The placement I ended up doing was packing Christmas stockings for cats which is what I said I did not want to do.

5.   EMPLOYERS

- People who go for a job interview should not be bullied by their boss and made to feel it's their fault if things go wrong at work. Employers should be more understanding towards their employee, especially disabled people as I was treated badly on my work placements and after I left and did voluntary work at the charity shop when someone new took over. Also, my husband was treated badly at his place of work.

- It is important not to ask a disabled person to carry a too heavy parcel or do something they do not have the strength for. It is wrong to tell a disabled student that they must be treated like everyone else because we all have different needs.

- Employers shouldn't tell their employees what their dress code should be when the disabled trainee wouldn't dream of telling them how to dress. The disabled employee may have conditions that require different shoes and clothes.

6.   DOCTORS/HOSPITALS

- Because of my experience in hospital while I was having Aidan and the fact that I did not get the help I needed because of my disability made me realise that other disabled people who are in the same situation should receive better care in the hospital while waiting to have their baby and that the hospital staff need to be better informed as to their special needs of a disabled mother looking after babies.

- Disabled mothers can be just as loving parents as other parents but may need extra help from a district nurse/midwife and the child or baby gets just as much love and attention as other children do proving that disabled mothers or fathers make good parents and deserve support.

7. DISABLED PEOPLE

- I thought that the Disability Discrimination Act was brought in to help disabled people to stop them from being discriminated against. Instead I find things are very different. I hope that the Discrimination Act is there to help all disabled people and that employers have to treat disabled people with the same rights as a person without a disability.

- I joined the local PHAB Club in Leamington where I made lots of friends, including Steve and we did lots of activities like dominoes, darts, cards and pool, going swimming and crafts and fireworks at the Rose and Crown pub next door and going on holiday once a year.

My experiences: a parental response

Bullying

It saddens me that I was unaware of the bullying Jane experienced in her first school – the only ordinary school she attended. I wish that I had explained to Jane that if you are bullied it is not your fault and told her very clearly that I would always help if it happened to her.

Even with young children teachers are not always aware that bullying is happening. Parents and professionals must seek to create an anti-bullying ethos, be vigilant and always listen sympathetically to a child who perceives him- or herself to be either bullying or bullied, and subsequently do something to change the situation.

'Ordinary' and 'special' schools

Jane was unhappy at ordinary school and happy at her special schools where she was able to make friends. Her abilities and disabilities were such that she would have been able to cope, with support, in a welcoming, inclusive ordinary school. This is a real dilemma for many parents of disabled children. On the one hand we believe in integration in principle, but fear it in practice for our vulnerable child. (See Chapter 3 in *Disability Voice: Towards an Enabling Education*, (Leicester 1998), published by Jessica Kingsley Publishers.) In my research into parental experience I discovered that all parents of disabled children recognised the benefits of integration (including for non-disabled children) but felt that ordinary schools needed to change – to be better resourced and (in a broad sense of the term) more accessible.

A specific area of learning disability

I feel hurt that so often in Jane's life her lack of number concepts was not sufficiently recognised and allowed for. In school she had a bad experience with 'hard sums'; in college she had a problem with laying the table and on training placements was in trouble for being late when her number problems clearly had implications for working out the time. I suggest that several of the bad experiences described by Jane show a lack of professionals' understanding of the extensive implications of her particular learning difficulty.

Jane's vegetarianism

Jane has described how and why she became a vegetarian (I am not a vegetarian). It was a moral choice which she has always maintained. Since childhood Jane has had a strong moral sense and strong compassion. This enables her to make sound moral judgements. The educational academic tendency to see moral development mainly in terms of cognitive ability misses, I think, the importance of our emotions of care, compassion and a feeling for justice.

Poor 'training' experiences

Jane experienced very poor training opportunities after college. If learning disabled people are to have employment prospects, with all that means in terms of social inclusion, good training is crucial.

In training, much emphasis is placed on 'independence'. This is important – provided we also recognise and value the interdependence of us all.

Parenthood

Disabled adults can sometimes experience social isolation. Jane has always appreciated people who chat to her, and are good listeners – 'nice to talk to'. PHAB (Physically Handicapped and Able-Bodied) was important to her for peer friendships, and it was there she met her husband-to-be, Stephen.

Stephen and Jane are the proud parents of a lovely, lively, flourishing son. As Jane said, she received inadequate support in hospital, those first crucial days after his birth.

For me, being a grandmother is a great joy, and as do many other grandparents, I enjoy providing a bit of supportive assistance to Jane and Aidan. Sadly, not all disabled mothers have family support and a high proportion of learning disabled parents have their children taken from them. This is a heartbreaking example of society's inadequate support for disabled people.

Appendix Two

Pictures to Colour

Tom's Famous Bridge

The Magic Shoe Box

A Kind Revenge

One and One Makes Trouble

Signs of Change

Gifts for Divali

Across the Pond

A Careless Boy